Beatrix Potter

WHO
WROTE
THAT?

Beatrix Potter

Margaret Speaker Yuan

Foreword by
Kyle Zimmer

CHELSEA HOUSE
PUBLISHERS
A Haights Cross Communications ✈ Company ®
Philadelphia

CHELSEA HOUSE PUBLISHERS

VP, New Product Development Sally Cheney
Director of Production Kim Shinners
Creative Manager Takeshi Takahashi
Manufacturing Manager Diann Grasse

Staff for BEATRIX POTTER

Executive Editor Matt Uhler
Editorial Assistant Sarah Sharpless
Production Editor Noelle Nardone
Photo Editor Sarah Bloom
Interior and Cover Designer Keith Trego
Layout 21st Century Publishing and Communications, Inc.

http://www.chelseahouse.com

A Haights Cross Communications ✦ Company ®

First Printing

1 3 5 7 9 8 6 4 2

Library of Congress Cataloging-in-Publication Data

Speaker-Yuan, Margaret.
  Beatrix Potter/Margaret Speaker-Yuan.
    p. cm.—(Who wrote that?)
  Includes bibliographical references and index.
  ISBN 0-7910-8655-0
  1. Potter, Beatrix, 1866–1943—Juvenile literature. 2. Authors, English—20th century—
Biography—Juvenile literature. 3. Artists—Great Britain—Biography—Juvenile literature.
4. Children's stories—Authorship—Juvenile literature. 5. Animals in literature—Juvenile
literature. 6. Animals in art—Juvenile literature. I. Title. II. Series.
PR6031.O72Z865 2005
823'.912—dc22
                                                          2005008183

All links and Web addresses were checked and verified to be correct at the time
of publication. Because of the dynamic nature of the Web, some addresses
and links may have changed since publication and may no longer be valid.

Table of Contents

FOREWORD BY
KYLE ZIMMER
PRESIDENT, FIRST BOOK

HUMANITY IS POWERED by stories. From our earliest days as thinking beings, we employed every available tool to tell each other stories. We danced, drew pictures on the walls of our caves, spoke, and sang. All of this extraordinary effort was designed to entertain, recount the news of the day, explain natural occurrences—and then gradually to build religious and cultural traditions and establish the common bonds and continuity that eventually formed civilizations. Stories are the most powerful force in the universe; they are the primary element that has distinguished our evolutionary path.

Our love of the story has not diminished with time. Enormous segments of societies are devoted to the art of storytelling. Book sales in the United States alone topped $26 billion last year; movie studios spend fortunes to create and promote stories; and the news industry is more pervasive in its presence than ever before.

There is no mystery to our fascination. Great stories are magic. They can introduce us to new cultures, or remind us of the nobility and failures of our own, inspire us to greatness or scare us to death; but above all, stories provide human insight on a level that is unavailable through any other source. In fact, stories connect each of us to the rest of humanity not just in our own time, but also throughout history.

This special magic of books is the greatest treasure that we can hand down from generation to generation. In fact, that spark in a child that comes from books became the motivation for the creation of my organization, First Book, a national literacy program with a simple mission: to provide new books to the most disadvantaged children. At present, First Book has been at work in hundreds of communities for over a decade. Every year children in need receive millions of books through our organization and millions more are provided through dedicated literacy institutions across the United States and around the world. In addition, groups of people dedicate themselves tirelessly to working with children to share reading and stories in every imaginable setting from schools to the streets. Of course, this Herculean effort serves many important goals. Literacy translates to productivity and employability in life and many other valid and even essential elements. But at the heart of this movement are people who love stories, love to read, and want desperately to ensure that no one misses the wonderful possibilities that reading provides.

When thinking about the importance of books, there is an overwhelming urge to cite the literary devotion of great minds. Some have written of the magnitude of the importance of literature. Amy Lowell, an American poet, captured the concept when she said, "Books are more than books. They are the life, the very heart and core of ages past, the reason why men lived and worked and died, the essence and quintessence of their lives." Others have spoken of their personal obsession with books, as in Thomas Jefferson's simple statement, "I live for books." But more compelling, perhaps, is the almost instinctive excitement in children for books and stories.

Throughout my years at First Book, I have heard truly extraordinary stories about the power of books in the lives of children. In one case, a homeless child, who had been bounced from one location to another, later resurfaced—and the only possession that he had fought to keep was the book he was given as part of a First Book distribution months earlier. More recently, I met a child who, upon receiving the book he wanted, flashed a big smile and said, "This is my big chance!" These snapshots reveal the true power of books and stories to give hope and change lives.

As these children grow up and continue to develop their love of reading, they will owe a profound debt to those volunteers who reached out to them—a debt that they may repay by reaching out to spark the next generation of readers. But there is a greater debt owed by all of us—a debt to the storytellers, the authors, who have bound us together, inspired our leaders, fueled our civilizations, and helped us put our children to sleep with their heads full of images and ideas.

WHO WROTE THAT? is a series of books dedicated to introducing us to a few of these incredible individuals. While we have almost always honored stories, we have not uniformly honored storytellers. In fact, some of the most important authors have toiled in complete obscurity throughout their lives or have been openly persecuted for the uncomfortable truths that they have laid before us. When confronted with the magnitude of their written work or perhaps the daily grind of our own, we can forget that writers are people. They struggle through the same daily indignities and dental appointments, and they experience the intense joy and bottomless despair that many of us do. Yet somehow they rise above it all to deliver a powerful thread that connects us all. It is a rare honor to have the opportunity that these books provide to share the lives of these extraordinary people. Enjoy.

Beatrix Potter (1866–1943) grew up in London but spent much of her adult life in the Lake District of England, where she owned farmland. This sign, painted by Potter of her well-known character, Peter Rabbit, can be found in downtown Glasmere, Lake District of England. Upon her death, the National Trust preserved the farm—Hill Top Farm—where Potter first lived away from her parents. The National Trust continues to maintain the cottage and gardens as well as looking after her furniture and china exactly as Potter had done during her life there.

1

First Book

BEATRIX POTTER OPENED the cover of a small book. She hoped that the book would meet her expectations. As she leafed through the pages, she examined the pictures carefully. The pictures were of four tiny rabbits. Three of the rabbits obediently went to pick blackberries as their mother requested. The fourth rabbit, the mischievous one, squeezed under the gate and into a neighbor's garden. Potter read the text and smiled. She had written and illustrated the book herself. It was her first time seeing her work in print.

For several years, Potter had tried to find a publishing company for her story. She had sent it out to six different publishers in the hope that one of them would buy the manuscript and publish it for her. Unfortunately, the publishing companies either rejected the manuscript altogether or wanted to change it more than Potter felt she could accept.

After the story had been returned to her by all six of the publishers, Potter decided to publish it herself. She hired a printer and paid for the book with her own money. Now, in December 1901, she held the first copy of *The Tale of Peter Rabbit*.

A VICTORIAN CHILDHOOD

Beatrix Potter was born on July 28, 1866. Both of her parents, Helen and Rupert Potter, came from families that had made their fortunes in the cotton business. Rupert had been educated as a barrister (a member of the English legal profession). He had inherited so much money from his parents, however, that he found he did not need to practice law or even to work at all. Rupert enjoyed reading, visiting art galleries, going to his club, or pursuing a recently invented hobby, photography. He and his family lived at Two Bolton Gardens, on the outskirts of Central London.

London in the 1860s and 1870s was a prosperous city with many new buildings being planned and constructed. Builders used the latest in high technology: the steel frame and the hydraulic elevator. The London Underground, the world's first subterranean railroad system, began to carry passengers in 1863. At that time London was the capital of the most powerful nation in the world, Great Britain. Britain ruled territories from Canada to India to Hong Kong. Queen Victoria, who took the throne in 1837, gave her name to the entire era (the Victorian Era) through her vast influence on style, manners, and customs.

Despite its prosperous surface, London nevertheless suffered from a number of problems, including crowded living conditions, crime, and disease. Children were not required by law to go to school. Laws against employing children did not exist. Wages were set by employers, with no set minimum wage required by law. There were no unions to negotiate how many hours one could work, how much one must be paid, or under what work conditions it was healthy to labor. Generally, people worked 10-hour days, six days a week. Despite working 60-hour weeks, many families were so poor that they had to send their children to work in order to afford food, clothing, and shelter for the entire family.

In contrast to Central London, the neighborhood of Bolton Gardens, located in South Kensington, consisted of brand-new, three- or four-story homes bought as soon as they were built by well-to-do middle-class families. The streets in South Kensington were rough and remained unpaved until the early 1880s. Gas lanterns were lit each evening to provide street lighting. The London Underground opened a station at Kensington, near Bolton Gardens, in 1868. The area, being close to Central London, made the cultural life of the city easily available for the Potter family. Yet the area was far enough away from the downtown area of London that issues such as poverty, disease, overcrowding, and lack of education were not visible to the families who lived in Bolton Gardens.

Potter's mother, Helen, spent her time paying visits, doing charity work, and running the Potter household. One of Helen's interests was transcribing books into Braille so that blind people could read them with their fingers. In the evenings, Helen and Rupert went to the theater, to the opera, or to the symphony. They often dined with friends, or hosted dinner parties at their home for their close circle of acquaintances. As was common during the Victorian Era, Helen hired servants to care for her children, in this case a nurse and governess. Children were not often included in the adult world, so Helen went about her daily activities without her daughter or her son, Bertram Potter.

Planning the family's social schedule and managing the household were Helen's main responsibilities. In the late 1800s, these activities required a considerable investment of both time and energy. Nine servants were employed to care for the Potter family and their home in Bolton Gardens. There was a cook, a butler, a parlor maid, a nurse, a coachman, and four under-servants who assisted the senior staff. To keep the four-story house clean, the maids used brooms, mops, dust cloths, soap, and water. There was no electricity, so there were no household machines to help with the labor—no automatic dish washers, no washing machines, no vacuum cleaners, and no food processors. All the work to clean, cook, wash, and iron was done by hand. As the mistress of the household, Helen hired the servants, approved the week's menus, paid the servants' wages, and oversaw the household budget. Although she was wealthy enough to be considered a lady of leisure, such women were still expected to run their families' homes. Helen's daily life was similar to running a small business.

Potter lived on the third floor of the house. Her room, called the nursery, was large and sunny, with windows overlooking the gardens and nearby park. She slept, played, and ate most of her meals in the nursery. A servant named McKenzie was in charge of her care. McKenzie was called a nurse even though she did not have any medical training.

From the time Potter was born, McKenzie looked after her, feeding her, changing her diapers, and rocking her to sleep at night. They went for walks in the garden, with Potter in a large baby carriage called a pram. As her only companion, McKenzie even helped Potter take her first steps.

After Potter learned to walk, she and McKenzie explored the park near the house together. Potter held McKenzie's hand while McKenzie taught her the names of all the flowers. She was not allowed to play with the other children in the park. Her parents were afraid that their daughter would catch colds or other more severe diseases from children she met at the park. In the days before antibiotics and immunizations, diseases such as measles, polio, diphtheria, or whooping cough killed many children. By isolating Potter from other children, Helen and Rupert thought they could prevent her from being exposed to life-threatening illnesses.

Once Potter was old enough to feed herself, McKenzie brought her meals up from the kitchen on a tray, but McKenzie no longer stayed to eat with her. As a servant, McKenzie was supposed to eat in the kitchen with the other servants. And so, Potter ate alone in the nursery.

Potter seldom saw her mother or father. They were always busy, paying calls during the day and going out in the evening. Occasionally, Potter's grandmother came to visit. Grandmother Potter always brought Piglette, a stuffed pig made of white flannelette, when she came.

Piglette was one of Potter's favorite toys. Another favorite toy was a wooden doll named Topsy. Piglette had to go home with Grandmother after a visit, but Topsy got to stay with Potter.

One day, Grandmother gave her granddaughter some news that was both sad and happy. McKenzie was going to be the nurse for another baby. The baby was Potter's brand-new brother, Bertram. While she was happy to have a baby brother, she was sad that McKenzie would be taking care of him instead of her. Now that she was almost 6 years old, Potter was old enough to begin learning how to read. However it had been decided that she would not go to school. A governess was hired to come live at Two Bolton Gardens. The governess was responsible for Potter's education.

Potter was not sure whether she liked the idea of having a governess. Lessons sounded boring and tedious. She did not know what to expect. A governess might be mean, strict, and unfriendly, or she might be kind and cheerful. There was no way to know beforehand what kind of person the governess was. The prospect of so many changes in her life made Potter nervous. Everyone—her grandmother, McKenzie, her mother, the entire household, it seemed— was so busy with the new baby that they had even less time to spend with her than they used to have. Perhaps, she thought, she might find someone, even a pet, to whom she could confide her fears and hopes.

PETS AND LESSONS

One morning soon after Bertram was born, Potter asked the butler, Mr. Cox, if he would give her a box. He asked what the box would contain. She told him that she planned to use it as a house for a mouse. When he asked where she would get the mouse, she suggested the kitchen. McKenzie had told her that the cook had plenty of mice in the kitchen.[1]

Mr. Cox promised to find a box and a mouse for Potter. In a few days, a knock came at the nursery door. Mr. Cox tiptoed into the room. He had crept up the stairs in his stocking feet, so that no one would hear him. He placed a box painted to look like a house on the table. From inside the box came a scratching noise. Potter peered into the house through a hole painted to look like a doorway. Inside, she saw a beautiful gray mouse. Potter named her Hunca Munca.

She played with Hunca Munca all day and put the mouse's box at the foot of her bed at night. Soon Hunca Munca was tame enough to eat tidbits from Potter's hand. Whenever Potter heard someone coming up the stairs to the nursery, she whisked Hunca Munca into her house, and hid the house in the cupboard.[2]

Did you know...

Beatrix Potter's privately printed copies of *The Tale of Peter Rabbit* have become collector's items. Copies of the book can bring in as much as 7,000 pounds sterling (over $13,000) at auction. The book in the Warne edition has sold over 40 million copies worldwide, in many languages. In 2005, the story was translated into a new language, Scots. Products based on the character of Peter Rabbit include china, tea sets, games, linens, soaps, medallions, jewelry, dolls, soft toys, rugs, wallpaper, lamps, baby items, and many more.

As Potter ate breakfast one morning soon after Hunca Munca's arrival in the nursery, a knock came at the door. Potter wondered who it could be. McKenzie never knocked. Surely no one else would have climbed the stairs to the nursery so early in the morning. Maybe it was the new governess. Potter scrambled to put Hunca Munca in her house, but before she could hide the house in the cupboard, the door to the nursery opened.

A young, friendly looking woman stood at the door. She introduced herself as Miss Hammond, the governess. She walked over to Potter and peered into Hunca Munca's house. She admired the house and asked who lived in it.

Potter told Miss Hammond the mouse's name. Miss Hammond smiled, and told Potter that she loved pets. As a child, she said she had even had a pet rabbit. His name had been Peter.[3]

Lessons with Miss Hammond were not tedious or boring the way Potter had feared. For one thing, she and Miss Hammond fixed up the schoolroom to suit them-selves, with storybooks spread out on a table, drawing supplies scattered next to the books, and Hunca Munca's house nestled next to the pens, pencils, and papers. Miss Hammond also encouraged Potter to draw animals and flowers from living models. Some of her early drawings showed Hunca Munca. Others showed cater-pillars, flowers, or birds. Miss Hammond made lessons fun through her sense of humor and her ability to engage her pupil's interest in drawing. She gave Potter her first box of paints.

Potter learned to read quickly. Her artistic talent made it easy for her to draw the letters of the alphabet. Arithmetic was not so easy for her. In fact, she wrote, "there is no general word to express the feelings I have always entertained towards arithmetic."[4]

Life for Potter was not only lessons. She and Miss Hammond went for long walks, where they found new flowers to draw. They went to the South Kensington Museum, now known as the Victoria and Albert Museum for Queen Victoria and her prince consort (the husband of a reigning queen) Prince Albert. There they looked at collections of fossils, insects, and skeletons. Potter took her sketchbook along whenever they visited the museums.

Sometimes Bertram and McKenzie joined Miss Hammond and Potter for walks in the garden. McKenzie pushed Bertram in his pram or let him crawl on the grass while Potter sketched. When he was old enough to walk, Bertram went along with Potter and Miss Hammond on their excursions to the park and the museums. His bed was moved into the nursery next to Potter's. He, too, enjoyed playing with Hunca Munca, who had acquired a husband named Appley Dappley.

Bertram's gentleness with the mice was noted by his sister and Miss Hammond. One day, they heard him shrieking. When they ran to him, they found him sitting up, watching Hunca Munca, who had just given birth to a litter of six babies on top of his blanket. He stared at the babies with delight, but he did not touch any of them. He seemed to know that touching the babies might injure them. Both Potter and Miss Hammond knew that Bertram was a most unusual baby.[5]

Unfortunately, Miss Hammond's mother became very ill. While the Potter family planned a vacation in Scotland, Miss Hammond told Potter that she would not be going with them. She had to go to Liverpool to nurse her mother back to health. Potter promised to write to Miss Hammond,

Beatrix Potter, pictured here, was born into a well-to-do family and lived in South Kensington, on the outskirts of London. Her interest in animals began when she was six years old. It was then that she got her first pet mouse, which she named Hunca Munca. Potter began to draw animals, flowers, and birds shortly thereafter.

and to send her sketches of the remarkable things Potter was sure to find in Scotland. The prospect of letters back and forth did not do much to comfort Potter. Miss Hammond had become a dear friend as well as a teacher.

SUMMERS IN THE COUNTRY

During the summer months, the Potter family and all the servants moved to a rented mansion in Scotland called Dalguise House. Traveling from London to Dalguise House meant that an omnibus (a horse-drawn carriage with seats that ran lengthwise) had to be hired. The omnibus carried the Potters, their servants, and the baggage from Two Bolton Gardens to Waterloo Station. At Waterloo, everyone in the Potter household boarded a train that would take them north, to the wild and rugged and very beautiful countryside of Scotland.

Rupert enjoyed both fishing and photography. He often caught huge salmon in the Tay River near Dalguise House. Many of his friends also liked the country life, including the painter John Everett Millais. Rupert and Millais were such good friends that Rupert photographed Millais in his studio. One of Rupert's photographs, that of William Gladstone, the British Prime Minister, was used by Millias as the basis for a portrait of Gladstone. In the summer, the subjects of Rupert's photographs were not limited to politicians, to his family, or to his friends. He also recorded his catch of the day by taking photographs of the fish.

Although Potter missed Miss Hammond, she had her brother as a playmate. The grounds at Dalguise House were full of wildlife. Potter sketched and drew the creatures, plants, and scenery, using the box of paints given to her by Miss Hammond. Potter and Bertram went on long walks with Mr. Cox, the butler, keeping watch over them. Sometimes McKenzie took them to visit her relatives who lived in the area. When they went visiting, the children and McKenzie were driven by the Potter family's coachman. They passed farms that had pigs, sheep, and goats running in the yards. For the first time, Potter saw wide hills, rivers, and fertile valleys instead of the rows of houses that she was used to seeing in London. Country life, with its fresh air and the freedom to run and play, appealed to Potter from her very first summer's visit.

Unfortunately, the summer too quickly came to an end. The Potter family returned to London, and Potter received a letter from Miss Hammond. The letter said that Miss Hammond had to remain with her mother in Liverpool and would not return to Bolton Gardens. Potter's parents did not engage a new governess for their daughter. Potter tried to continue her studies on her own, reading, writing, and sketching. McKenzie often walked Potter to the South Kensington Museum, where she studied the specimens in their cases. She had a special friend at the Museum, Miss Woodward, who taught her anatomy and biology.

When Helen found out that Potter knew more about the bones, stomachs, and hearts of animals than about embroidery, she was horrified. She tried to stop the lessons, but Potter insisted. Embroidery, to Potter, was unbelievably boring. Sketching and learning were the only things she took pleasure from, and she hungered for them with a passion. Helen, in the face of her daughter's determination to continue visiting the museum, relented at last, and allowed the anatomy lessons to continue.

In the spring, Potter received a wonderful surprise. One day a knock came at the nursery door. Wondering, just as she had a year ago, who was knocking so early, Potter went to the door. In walked Miss Hammond. Potter's beloved governess had returned. Potter was overjoyed. Miss Hammond's mother was greatly improved in her health. Lessons began again, even the dreaded arithmetic exercises. The other lessons, however, were just as enjoyable as they had been in the past. Potter's days were full of learning, sketching, and painting.

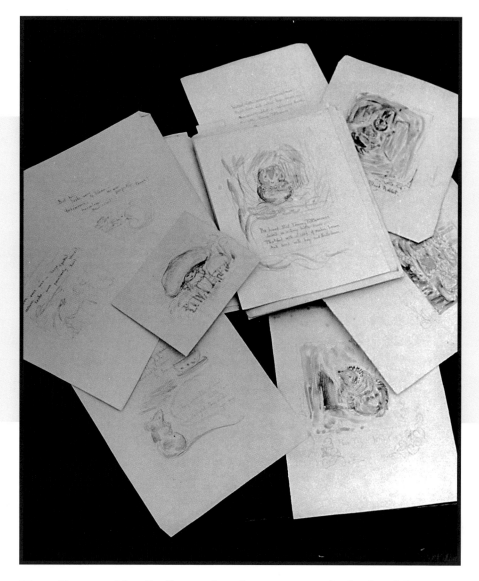

Young Potter and her family vacationed every summer in the Scottish country-side, where she enjoyed spending time outdoors. The great outdoors provided inspiration to the budding writer, and Potter began to make up stories about her many outdoor pets—rabbits, mice, frogs, a hedgehog, and even a bat were all subjects for Potter's stories. Potter even drew detailed pictures of her pets. Some of these drawings were preserved and are pictured here.

2

Pets and Painting

LIFE FOR THE Potter family entered a routine that would last for 10 years, from 1871 to 1881. The family spent their winters at Two Bolton Gardens and their summers in Scotland. Each location boasted different types of activities for Bertram and Potter. During their summers, the children found pets, ran outdoors, and collected treasures. The only drawback to Potter's enjoyment of her summers was that Miss Hammond usually went to care for her mother in Liverpool rather than accompanying the family to Scotland. However, during the winter, Miss Hammond returned to give Potter her lessons.

As a child, Potter's health was not strong. She often suffered from colds and headaches. She had no playmates or young friends other than her brother and the occasional companionship of various cousins. For company, Potter kept a number of pets, from rabbits to rats, mice, and even a bat. Bertram shared her enthusiasm for animals. The mouse Hunca Munca and her husband Appley Dappley had many generations of descendants. Sometimes the children brought pets back from their summers in Scotland. Other times they bought animals at local pet shops. They owned a frog named Punch, a pair of lizards called Toby and Judy, and a ring-snake known as Sally. Potter had two particular favorite pets. One was a rabbit called Benjamin Bouncer. The other was a hedgehog named Tiggy Winkle. Both of them became favorite subjects for Potter's sketches.

In the summertime, Potter's health improved. With fresh air, the change of scenery, and the freedom to go on walks, she was ill far less often. The better nutrition of the country, such as an unlimited supply of fresh milk and eggs, may also have been a health benefit for her. She and Bertram wandered the countryside. They made friends with the collies at a nearby farmyard. They fed grain to the chickens, and soft mash to the ducklings. They collected eggs in a basket, and brought home flowers, from snapdragons to pelargonium to heather.

One summer in Scotland, they found a dead fox. In secret, they skinned and boiled it so that they could perch the skeleton on a stand. They drew the fox's skeleton, as well as every other specimen they could find. They discovered an obsolete printing press, and made a concoction of soot and oil to serve as the ink. When they printed a series of artistic labels for the jam pots, they made such a mess that the printing press was confiscated.

Potter made up stories about her pets, and gave them personalities as well as names. She often drew very detailed pictures of them, sometimes in pencil, sometimes in pen, ink, and watercolor. When she went on nature walks in the countryside, she often brought back flowers to draw. Her sketchbooks from as early as 9 years old demonstrate an exquisite command of line and perspective. Her sketches also showed a love of fantasy animals that became a part of her work as an adult. Often, she drew her pets in human situations, dressing a rabbit in a bonnet and mantle (cloak), wrapping a muffler (scarf) around the neck of a newt, or giving a fishing pole to a frog.

For her reading material, Potter had a number of books. The Potter family owned a complete set of the novels of Sir Walter Scott. Potter learned to read using tales such as *Ivanhoe*. This was the story of a stalwart Crusader who helped Richard the Lionhearted escape from the plots of his evil brother, King John. Another story was a brand-new publication, privately printed by an Oxford professor of mathematics named Charles Lutwidge Dodgson. Dodgson used the pen name of Lewis Carroll; the book was *Alice in Wonderland*. Potter reported later that she was so absorbed in the pictures by the illustrator John Tenniel that she barely remembered reading the story.[6] Potter described herself as looking like one of Tenniel's drawings. She wrote, "What I wore was absurdly uncomfortable; white *piqué* starched frocks just like Tenniel's *Alice in Wonderland*, and cotton stockings striped round like zebra's legs, black velvet on Sundays, and either black or brown ribbon week days . . . I remember the bands fastened with a bit of elastic, looped over a button behind the ear; it hurt."[7]

Many friends visited the Potter family in Scotland. In London, where entertaining was strictly formal, the children were not allowed into the drawing room. They were expected to stay upstairs, in the nursery. However, on vacations in Scotland, formal rules were relaxed and the children were allowed to mingle with their parents' guests. Some of the guests were very fond of Potter. Potter knitted a woolen scarf for her favorite, Mr. William Gaskill. Mr. Gaskill visited the Potters every summer for over a decade. Later in life, Potter remembered his friendship and his interest in her pets and her drawings.

When he turned 11, Bertram was sent away to boarding school, but Potter stayed home. For Potter, the lack of schooling was both good and bad. Although she missed Bertram's companionship, she loved to draw and paint more than ever. Miss Hammond was able to work with her one-on-one; there were no other students to take time away from Potter's studies as there would have been if she had also been sent to school. Instead, Potter was allowed to learn her dreaded arithmetic facts at her own pace.

Although she did not have friends or playmates, she had time to draw. Potter later wrote, "Thank goodness my education was neglected; I was never sent to school . . . The reason I am glad I did not go to school—it would have rubbed off some of the originality (if I had not died of shyness or been killed with over pressure). I fancy I could have been taught anything if I had been caught young; but it was in the days when parents kept governesses, and only boys went to school in most families."[8]

Although later in life Potter was glad not to have been sent to school, her parents were merely obeying the customs of their social class. They did not keep her home from

Beatrix Potter never had a formal education, as it was not the custom for women at the time to go to school. Instead, she was taught by a governess at home. Fortunately, Potter's first governess took great interest in her talent for drawing. In her teens, Potter also studied art more formally with several teachers. This is a photograph of Potter when she was 15 years old.

school because of a sympathetic understanding of her needs. She did not go to school because, being a girl, she was expected to have different goals and prospects than her brother.

In the late nineteenth century, boys often received a formal education while girls did not. Most people thought that well-to-do girls like Potter only needed to know how to dance, sing, and make pleasant conversation. Girls were not expected to follow a career, or to have to work to support themselves. In fact, girls were not allowed to attend classes at universities, vote, or hold property in their own names. Until the Married Women's Property Act in 1882, women lost all rights to their own property when they married. Everything a woman owned, even land she had bought herself, became her husband's property. A husband could sell a house that his wife had owned before her marriage. He did not have to give her any of the proceeds from the sale. He was legally entitled to keep all of his wife's money for himself.

Voting rights and educational equality came much later than the right to retain property after marriage. Limited suffrage (the right to vote) was enacted for some British women in 1918. That same year, the first woman was elected to Parliament (Britain's ruling body, similar to the United States Congress). Women were allowed to take classes at some universities, but they were not awarded degrees at the end of their studies. Women were not allowed to teach at the university level. Without degrees, it was difficult for women to become doctors, lawyers, or engineers. Later in life, when Potter became interested in science, her lack of formal training proved to be a handicap. Because she was a girl, she was not allowed to study for a degree in science. Her drawings and experiments on mushrooms and fungi were not given the credibility they deserved.

With Bertram away at school, Potter turned her attention even more to art. She took drawing lessons with several teachers, one of whom taught her how to paint with oils. Her preference, because of the linseed oil's sticky, unpleasant texture, was to work in watercolors. Her drawings for her teachers showed attention to technical details such as light and shadow. However, they lacked the sense of movement and life that her drawings of animals possessed.

Potter's beloved governess, Miss Hammond, stopped working for the Potter family the year Bertram went to school. Potter considered herself, at nearly 17 years old, to be too mature to need another governess. Her parents, however, decided it best to replace Miss Hammond with a new governess, Annie Carter. Although she remained for only three years as Potter's governess, Annie proved to be a lifelong friend. She married when she left the Potter household. Her children became Potter's first audience, the first recipients of the illustrated letters that Potter called picture letters.

After 10 years of vacations in Scotland, the family's favorite summer home, Dalguise House, became unavailable. The Potter family went instead to the Lake District, an area of hills, streams, and numerous lakes. Some of the highest mountains in England were in the Lake District. The family rented a castle near the town of Wray near Lake Windermere. Lake Windermere, one of the most beautiful lakes in England, had been celebrated by the poet William Wordsworth. In the Lake District, the Potter family first met a man by the name of Hardwicke Rawnsley, who was the canon (Anglican priest) of Wray.

Rawnsley and his wife Edith became Potter's close friends. Rawnsley was an avid naturalist who devoted much of his energy to preserving farmland in the Lake

District. Because of its great natural beauty, the area was in danger of being developed for vacation homes on a large scale. Rawnsley had founded the Lake District Defense Society, an association that fought development. Later, he became involved in the formation of the National Trust, a society that preserved Britain's heritage both in agriculture and architecture. Edith was a teacher and a prolific painter. Together they had founded a school of industrial arts to preserve traditional handicrafts in the face of rapid industrialization. They encouraged Potter's drawing and writing. Rawnsley was himself a published poet, and the author of a book for children, *Moral Verses for the Young*. His friendship proved invaluable to Potter when she began to look for a way to publish her stories.

Potter became closer to her father, Rupert, during her late teens and early twenties. Together they visited many museums and art galleries. Rupert retained his interest in photography, often posing his children in the garden. He gave Potter one of his old cameras to use. She complained that he only let her lug it about because it was so heavy that he no longer wanted to carry it.

Potter's mother, however, remained distant. She often found fault with her daughter for wanting to visit Annie and her children. Potter wrote, "my mother will not order the carriage in the morning or make up her mind, and if I say I should like to go out after lunch I am keeping her in, and if she does not go and I have missed the chance of a long drive, it is provoking."[9]

About this time, Potter began to keep a journal in code. The code was not deciphered until 1958. Many of the journals were kept at the farm where Potter lived later in life. Potter's cousin, Caroline Hutton Clarke, donated the journals to a collector of Potter memorabilia and books named Leslie Linder. Linder spent years poring over Potter's tiny writing without deciphering the key to her code. One evening, as he was about to give up forever, he saw on one of the pages the Roman numerals XVI, and the number 1793. Thinking that 1793 might be the year 1793, he looked in a reference work, the *Dictionary of Dates*. Nothing was listed in that work, so he looked in a children's encyclopedia. He found an entry that read, "Louis XVI, French King; born Versailles 1754; guillotined Paris 1793."[10]

Did you know...

Beatrix Potter kept pets throughout her life. At various times, she owned mice, a bat, guinea pigs, rabbits, hedgehogs, dogs, squirrels, rats, and pigs; however, she was never fond of cats. Even when a rat that she called Samuel Whiskers tore off the wallpaper in her study, at least as high as he could reach, she was reluctant to have a cat in the house to kill him. Only when her farm manager's wife insisted did Potter begin to keep cats in order to control the mice and rats, and to keep them out of the house. Yet Potter's attitude towards animals was somewhat contradictory. During World War II, she bred rabbits to use as food for her dogs, in the anticipation that dog food would be hard to come by. Similarly, when some of the Girl Guides who camped on her land looked overly thin to the point of appearing malnourished, she had a sheep butchered so that they could have some meat.

Laboring with a magnifying glass, Linder determined that one of the words in the line with the Roman numerals and the year was the word "execution." By midnight, Linder had created a cipher key, that is, a list of Potter's symbols with their corresponding letters in the alphabet. Linder spent the next five years translating the journals, which were first published in 1966.

Why Potter kept the journals in code has never been determined. She may have known about Leonardo da Vinci's coded journals. Almost certainly, she knew that the famous English diarist, Samuel Pepys, kept his private journal in code, even though he later translated them into English and published them. Possibly she was concerned that her privacy might be violated, as servants or her parents might read her diary if she had kept it in an uncoded form. In any case, once they were deciphered, Potter's journals revealed her daily life as she ended her teenage years and entered her twenties.

Potter's days included visits to relatives and friends, to museums, and to social events. She recorded and commented on the politics of the day. There were violent demonstrations by the unemployed, which she recorded in her journal. Nothing, however, served to keep her at home. Even explosions, such as a series of bombings by supporters of Home Rule (people who wanted Ireland to be separated politically from Britain), did not stop her from going to the theater. Her travels with her parents were described, with the prices of the fares, and how long it took them to reach their destinations. She noted which of her pets traveled with her, all carefully concealed in hutches or special carrying cages. Usually, her companions were Benjamin Bouncer or, after Benjamin's death, a rabbit called Peter Piper (also known simply as Peter

Rabbit); Tiggy Winkle, a hedgehog; and one of Hunca Munca's descendents.

Potter's journal records deaths, funerals, and illnesses, as was the history of the family. Potter made lengthy comments on art exhibitions she visited, analyzing the techniques used by the painters and discussing what she liked, or disliked, about the works. Her days appeared full of activity, but there is no mention of love or romance or even of close friendships. In one of her few entries about companionship, she noted that Annie Carter was about the youngest person she had known.[11]

Potter's journal showed that she was very ill for several years. She had rheumatic fever, an acute inflammatory disease that followed a streptococcus infection. In the days before antibiotics, rheumatic fever could not be cured. The only treatment was to let the illness run its course, and to try to treat the symptoms. In her journal, Potter described how her joints ached and how her physician feared that her heart valves had been damaged. In her entry for March 28, 1885, she wrote:

> A lamentable falling off. Had my few remaining locks clipped
> short at Douglas's. Draughty. My hair nearly all came off since
> I was ill. Now that the sheep is shorn, I may say without pride
> that I have seldom seen a more beautiful head of hair than
> mine. Last summer it was very thick and within about four
> inches of my knees, being more than a yard long.[12]

Despite the severity of her illness, Potter eventually recovered her strength. She returned to her usual pursuits of attending art exhibits, writing letters, and traveling. Her travels, however, were seldom without her parents. When she went to visit her cousin, Caroline Hutton (later Caroline Hutton Clarke, who gave Potter's diaries to Leslie Linder), she wrote, "I had not been away independently for five years. It was an event."[13] Part of the charm, besides the novelty of traveling by herself, was the companionship of a woman about her own age. They talked about many subjects, from religion to marriage to old stories.

One evening, Caroline told her an anecdote about a local tailor. He had been working late one night, but was unable to finish a beautiful waistcoat that he was supposed to deliver in the morning. Exhausted, he left his workshop and went home. Next day, upon his return to work, he found the coat finished, except for one buttonhole. A note scrawled on a scrap of paper was thrust through one remaining buttonhole. In tiny letters, the note read, "No more twist."[14] Twist was the special kind of twine used to finish off buttonholes.

The story captivated Potter. In fact, when she went into Gloucester with her cousin's family, she asked where the tailor had his shop. When they pointed out the street, Potter immediately began to sketch. She pulled a button off her jacket, in order to have an excuse to visit a tailor. While the man sewed the button back on, she observed the workroom, noting many details. The story and the setting would stay in Potter's imagination for many years.

Although she was a grown woman, Potter did not have her own income. Her financial support came entirely from her parents. They expected her to remain with them most of the time, particularly as they grew older and their health, mainly her father's, began to fail.

Bertram, sympathetic to his sister's needs, found a way for her to make some money. He contacted a publisher on her behalf. He sent Potter's pictures to a new type of venture, a greeting card firm. Because of advances in printing technology, colored greeting cards had become affordable.

Many cards were being published. Bertram took his sister's drawings of Benjamin Bouncer to the firm of Hildesheimer & Faulkner. On May 14, 1890, Potter received a fat letter from Bertram. In her journal, she wrote:

> The envelope contained a check for 6 pounds . . . and a very civil letter from the publisher . . . requiring me to send some more sketches.
>
> My first act was to give Bounce [Benjamin Bouncer] . . . a cupful of hemp seeds, the consequence being that when I wanted to draw him next morning he was partially intoxicated and wholly unmanageable. Then I retired to bed and lay awake chuckling . . .[15]

Potter sold several sets of drawings to different firms. She illustrated a book for another writer, *The Happy Pair* by Frederick Weatherly. Being paid for her work gave her great delight. She wrote, "It is something to have a little money to spend on books and to look forward to being independent."[16]

In 1892, the Potter family returned to Scotland for their summer holiday. As always, Potter wrote about her daily walks in her journal. On August 20, she noted:

> After breakfast taking Mr. Benjamin Bunny to pasture at the edge of the cabbage bed with his leather dog-lead, I heard a rustling, and out came a little wild rabbit to talk to him, it crept half across the cabbage bed and then sat up on its hind legs, apparently grunting. I replied, but the stupid Benjamin did nothing but stuff cabbage. The little animal evidently a female . . . advanced to . . . the other side of my rabbit, its face twitching with excitement and admiration for the beautiful Benjamin, who at length caught sight of it round a cabbage, and immediately bolted.[17]

In Scotland, Potter found a new hobby, that of mycology, or the study of fungi. The local postman, Charles McIntosh, was an expert on the natural history of the countryside. He observed the plants and animals during the hours he spent on his letter-carrying rounds. He provided Potter with many specimens to draw, and complimented her on the accuracy with which she depicted minute details of mosses and fungi. During the winter in London, Potter worked on organizing her drawings. She classified and identified the specimens so that she could categorize them scientifically. She hoped to use her drawings to illustrate a book on the subject of fungi.

Before she worked on the book, however, Potter's uncle, Sir Henry Roscoe, encouraged her to write and illustrate a scientific paper on spores of moulds. Roscoe was a chemist with numerous connections to the scientific societies of the day. Potter prepared her paper, which he checked minutely. He also introduced her to the Director of the Royal Botanical Gardens, believing that her discoveries were valuable original scientific work. The director, however, treated Potter as an amateur. Her lack of formal training in science made her work lack credibility in a world where advanced degrees were the norm. Although later her theories were proved to be correct, her amateur status meant that she was not taken seriously.

Annoyed by the lack of consideration for Potter's work, Uncle Henry submitted her paper to the Linnean Society, one of the foremost organizations devoted to the study of biology in the world. Her paper, with her theories about how spores of moulds propagated, was read before the society. Potter, however, was not present at the reading. Ladies were not allowed to attend the Linnean Society meetings.

Potter continued to draw moulds and spores, but she realized that the world of scientific illustration was closed to her. Influenced by the work of Randolph Caldecott, she decided to work on children's books. Caldecott had been one of the first artists who worked in the new field of children's illustration. He had died an untimely death at the age of 40 in 1886. Despite his short career, he was very influential, and was considered a pioneer in the field. During his lifetime, his books had sold over 876,000 copies. Potter's friend, Hardwicke Rawnsley; her uncle, Sir Henry Roscoe; and her brother Bertram, all encouraged her to write and draw for children.

Above is an original illustration from Beatrix Potter's book The Tailor of Gloucester, published in 1903. Potter heard the tale of an overworked tailor in Gloucester, whose assistants secretly completed his workload, from her cousin Caroline Hutton. Potter "retold" this tale, using mice as the tailor's assistants.

3

Publishing Success

ON SEPTEMBER 2, 1893, Potter wrote a letter to Noel Moore, Annie Carter's son. He had been ill for several months. Potter wrote to him frequently, to cheer him up during his long recovery. The letter began:

My dear Noel, I don't know what to write to you, so I shall tell you a story about four little rabbits whose names were—Flopsy, Mopsy, Cottontail and Peter.

They lived with their mother in a sand bank under the root of a big fir tree.

"Now, my dears," said old Mrs. Bunny, "you may go into the field or down the lane, but don't go into Mr. McGregor's garden."

Flopsy, Mopsy and Cottontail, who were good little rabbits went down the lane to gather blackberries, but Peter, who was very naughty, went straight away to Mr. McGregor's garden and squeezed underneath the gate."[18]

Another picture letter, addressed to Noel's sister Freda, told the story of the tailor that Potter had originally heard from her cousin, Caroline Hutton. The sewing, in Potter's version of the story, was done by the mice who lived in the tailor's shop.

Although she had few friends her own age, Potter was very close to Annie's children. As the years went by, Annie had six children: Noel, Eric, Marjorie, Winifrede (Freda), Norah, and Joan. Potter went to see them as often as she could. When she was away from London and could not visit, she wrote to them. Her letters to them were full of drawings, even ones that did not contain actual stories. All the Moore children treasured Potter's letters and kept them safely stored away, tied up in bundles with yellow ribbons.

Potter continued to live with her parents. Although she was nearly 30 years old, she was still unmarried. Young women of Potter's social class did not have their own households, as it was considered scandalous for unmarried women to live without a husband, a father, or a brother to act as head of the family. A girl generally went from her parents' home directly to her husband's, without ever living on her own. The Married Women's Property Act had given women control of their money and property after marriage. However, the social structure of the time discouraged women from becoming independent, either financially or intellectually.

Potter not only lived with her parents, she also nursed them whenever they became ill. Her journals contain frequent passages about her parents' health, noting tooth aches, colds, kidney stones, gout attacks, and the difficulty of nursing them.

> Mamma was taken very ill, sick from eight on Monday morn-ing till three next morning. If it had gone on longer I should have been frightened as there began to be a hemorrhage, but it stopped as suddenly as it began. She was upstairs nearly a fortnight, mending . . . I had a weary time, bother with the Servants as well. There is supposed to be some angelic senti-ment in tending the sick, but personally I should not associate angels with castor oil and emptying slops . . . Having been indoors almost continually, I caught a violent cold in my head, and my father being troubled with gravel [kidney stones] again, and every prospect of a hard winter, I have become lower than is the habit with me, a cheerful person.[19]

In the spring of 1895, Potter's father gave her a present that became significant when she decided to publish her own books. Potter wrote, "My father gave me a rather extraordinary present, certain Bonds of the North Pacific Railway which have paid no interest since April '93, the company being in the hands of [bankruptcy] receivers."[20] Potter made 100 pounds from the sale of the bonds, which she put into a savings account. It was the largest sum of money that she had ever possessed.

As she had done all her life, Potter spent her summers with her family in rented country homes. In 1896, Rupert chose a home near the village of Sawrey in the Lake District for his family's summer vacation. The home overlooked

Esthwaite Water. A watercolor picture of the view from the house towards the lake, done by Potter (undated, but probably painted in 1896), showed the lake surrounded by gentle rolling hills. A series of crags led to a bluff on the far side of the lake. Mountains loomed in the far distance beyond the crags. Trees and a cleared field appeared in the near distance. In the lower right corner, a wall lined with hollyhocks and a brick storage building complete the picture. As Potter had written in 1892, the first time she saw the lake, "I prefer a pastoral landscape backed by mountains. I have often been laughed at for thinking Esthwaitewater the most beautiful of the Lakes. It really strikes me that some scenery is almost theatrical, or ultra-romantic."[21]

After her stay in Sawrey in 1896, Potter wrote:

It is as nearly perfect a little place as I ever lived in . . . Perhaps my most sentimental leave-taking was with Don, the great farm collie. He came up and muddied me as I was packing up Peter Rabbit at the edge of dark. I accompanied him to the stable-gate, where he turned, holding it open with his side, and gravely shook hands. Afterwards, putting his paws solemnly on my shoulder, he licked my face and then went away into the farm.[22]

The farm she mentioned was called Hill Top Farm.

Bertram also accompanied the family on summer vacations. He had briefly studied at Oxford University, but had not done well academically. He suffered from alcoholism, which was partly responsible for his poor performance in school. Most of his time in Oxford had been spent painting and drinking, rather than studying. During the summer in Sawrey, Potter wrote about her walks with her brother in the countryside. They seemed as happy as they had been when they were children.

The year 1896 was the year Potter turned 30 years old. As always, she was far happier during her summers in the country than she was in London in the winter. She wrote, "A perfect, hot summer day, cloudless, but evening when it rolled up like thunder . . . I am thirty this day . . . I feel much younger at thirty than I did at twenty; firmer and stronger both in mind and body."[23]

Did you know...

Some of Beatrix Potter's works featured mischievous rabbits, rude squirrels, and disobedient kittens, who got into trouble because of their own naughtiness. Other works showed villains who took advantage of frivolous or careless creatures. One such villain was the elegantly dressed gentleman in *The Tale of Jemima Puddle-Duck*, who turned out to be a fox. The fox's interest in Jemima was culinary, and he was such a rascal that he had Jemima bring an onion and some sage with her to one of their meetings—an onion and sage that would be used to season the roast duck he enjoyed. Another villain was Samuel Whiskers, who tried to bake Tom Kitten into a pie. Few villains, however, could match the dastardly cook in *The Tale of Little Pig Robinson*. Not only did the cook lure Pig Robinson onto his ship, *The Pound of Candles*, he also fattened Robinson up on porridge and potatoes. Like the witch in *Hansel and Gretel*, he intended to make a meal, or a series of meals, from Pig Robinson after he was fat enough.

Potter had written about her desire to become independent, but her attempts to find more commissions for her drawings were slow to bear fruit. She had made some sales in 1890, but for 10 years, during the time she made her studies of fungi, she had very little success selling her work. Her friend Annie Moore, formerly Annie Carter, suggested that Potter might turn some of the picture letters she had written to Annie's children into books. In 1900, seven years after Potter had sent her picture letter to Noel, she asked him to return it to her. She thought it would make the basis for an illustrated book for children. She prepared a manuscript, with a black-and-white, pen-and-ink drawing on each page. The facing page had the text of the story. With the help of her friend, Hardwicke Rawnsley, she sent it to a number of publishers. When she received rejection after rejection of her story about Peter Rabbit, Rawnsley rewrote the story in verse. They hoped that telling the story in verse would make it more attractive to a potential publisher. Children's poems (like Edward Lear's *The Pelican Chorus* and *The Owl and the Pussycat,* as well as a book of verse by Rawnsley himself, *Moral Rhymes for the Young*) were very popular.

One publisher did show some interest in Potter's original, non-verse book, but he wanted to change the book's size. Potter had planned on publishing small books, ones that would be affordable. Writing about herself in the third person, she noted, "Miss Potter will go off to another publisher soon! She would rather make two or three little books costing 1 [shilling] each than one big book costing 6 [shillings] because she thinks little rabbits cannot afford to spend 6 shillings on one book."[24]

The currency at the time was the pound sterling. A pound was divided into 20 shillings; each shilling was made up of 12 pence (pennies). Skilled workers, such as shipwrights, builders, or stonemasons, earned about 40 shillings per week. A day's bread for a family of four, in a time when most workers ate a pound of bread a day, cost about a shilling. As far as books went, a family might own a Bible, and possibly one or two other books. Books for children were a new idea. At one shilling, Potter's book would cost about the same amount as a day's worth of bread for a poor working family. Most of the books would be bought by families that were more well-to-do than the working poor, but even so, a book would be considered a Christmas treat by most families, to be read aloud and treasured.

Potter decided to publish the book herself. She asked one of her old friends, Miss Woodward from the South Kensington Museum, for advice about printers. Miss Woodward came from a family of artists. Her father was the editor of *The Geographic Magazine*. One of her sisters had illustrated a number of children's books. Miss Woodward was able to advise Potter about printing and engraving. She recommended a printer called Strangeways & Sons. There were many different printing options to consider, such as whether to include color illustrations, how big the book should be, how many copies to print, and what kind of paper she should use. Potter decided to print the book in black and white, with a colored frontispiece (first page). She wanted a small book, one that children could hold easily. Her text was very simple, with one or two sentences per page. The text appeared on one page, with an illustration on the page facing the text. The book, in fact, was very much like the original picture letter Potter had sent to Noel. She added a few drawings, and made the story slightly longer.

The most expensive part of the project was the colored frontispiece, which was printed separately from the rest of

Beatrix Potter's books proved very popular with children and usually sold out immediately after release. Over the last 100 years, there have been more than 40 million copies of various editions of The Tale of Peter Rabbit; *one edition is shown above. According to* Publisher's Weekly, The Tale of Peter Rabbit *is the second best-selling children's book of all time in the United States.*

the book. Color printing came from a different printing press. Potter realized, when she looked at the costs, that it would be less expensive to print extra copies of the colored page on the first run than to reprint it later if she wanted to print more books. Her initial print run was 250 copies of the book, with an additional 250 copies of the frontispiece. The engraving and printing of the book cost 11 pounds.[25]

The first copies of her book were ready on December 16, 1901. In its first few weeks, Potter reported that she had made about 12 or 14 pounds by selling copies to her relatives and friends at one shilling, two pence per copy. Sir Arthur Conan Doyle, the author of the Sherlock Holmes stories, bought a copy for his children. In February 1902, she brought out a second edition with a print run of 200 books.[26]

On the same day that Potter received her privately printed books, on December 16, 1901, one of the publishers who had received Rawnsley's version of *The Tale of Peter Rabbit* in verse contacted Beatrix. The Frederick Warne Company offered to publish the second edition of *The Tale of Peter Rabbit*, if only Beatrix would redo the illustrations in color, and if she would rewrite the book in plain text, not in verse.

Potter agreed to the suggestions made by Harold Warne, the senior partner of the firm that his father, Frederick (now retired from the business) had founded. He offered her a contract, with royalties of one penny per each book. She wrote back that she would forego the royalty in order to keep the price of the books at one pound, six pence. She also asked for a clarification on who would hold copyright, always an important issue for a writer. Over the course of the negotiations, she visited the publisher at their offices in Bedford Street. She met not only Harold Warne, but also his brothers, William Fruing Warne and Norman Warne.

Norman's specialty in the firm was production, that is, in the printing and binding of the firm's books. He also was the book traveler, as sales representatives were called. He traveled to book shops in England and Ireland, selling books from the Frederick Warne Company catalog to the shop owners.

The Warnes and Potter agreed on a contract, which was signed in June 1902. There were two simultaneous editions of the book, with a print run of 8,000. The first 6,000 copies were bound in paperboard, and cost one shilling. Potter received no royalties on these copies in the first printing from Warne. The additional 2,000 copies were bound in cloth, and sold for one shilling, six pence. Potter received a 10 percent royalty (10 percent of the cover price) on these copies.

That spring, in April, while the negotiations for the contract and discussions about the drawings were taking place, Potter had gone with her brother to Kalemouth, in Scotland. As a young man, Bertram had traveled frequently to Scotland on sketching trips. He was generally accompanied only by a servant on these trips. Part of the servant's duties included keeping an eye on how much Bertram drank. Originally, Bertram had rented part of a house when he visited Scotland. One year he met a young woman named Mary Scott, who was helping in the house. They fell in love but there was a problem. Since she was of the servant class, he knew that his parents would forbid him from marrying her. However, in Scotland, the marriage laws were different from those in England. Bertram and Mary were able to marry secretly, without his parents' permission or knowledge. He bought a farm, and lived with her there, without telling his parents.

Potter made no mention of his marriage in any of her letters. Her journals ended in 1897, although it was possible that the later journals were lost. She wrote to her publisher from Bertram's farm in April and May 1902. Her letters were full of reports about the pictures she was in the process of completing for the publication of *The Tale of Peter Rabbit*. She was dissatisfied with some of the sketches. She wrote, "'Peter' died, at 9 years old, just before I began the drawings & now . . . I have got another young rabbit, & the drawings look wrong."[27]

Potter made changes in both the text and the drawings until the very last minute. The book went to press in the fall of 1902. Despite her doubts about the quality of the drawings and the text, the entire print run of 8,000 books was sold out before the books became available on October 2, 1902.

With the success of her books, Beatrix Potter was able to purchase Hill Top Farm near the village of Sawrey, in the Lake District. Although she came from an upper-class family, Potter didn't want to be a refined country lady. She was not afraid to get her hands dirty while tending her own sheep, horses, and pigs. Here, Potter is pictured at Hill Top Farm with one of her herding dogs.

4

Hilltop Farm and the Lake Country

POTTER GAVE HER opinion of *The Tale of Peter Rabbit* when she wrote, "It is much more satisfactory to address a real live child. I often think that was the secret of the success of *Peter Rabbit*; it was written to a child—not made to order."[28]

In his analysis of children's fantasy books, *The Natural History of Make-Believe*, critic and literary historian John Goldthwaite agreed with Potter. He wrote, "Beatrix Potter's humble sand-bank [where the Bunny family lived] must stand out as one of the paramount addresses along the passage of story from folklore to modern children's tale . . . the kind of intimate book that is at once a mature work of empathic art and unmistakably, and once and for all, a book for young children."[29]

While she was working on the final drawings and text of *The Tale of Peter Rabbit*, Potter decided to privately publish another of her story letters. The story was based on the vignette (brief story) that her cousin Caroline Hutton had told her concerning a tailor. The tale was similar to the fable *The Elves and the Shoemaker*, where shoes left over-night in the workshop were completed by elves. In Potter's story, *The Tailor of Gloucester*, a tailor worked late on Christmas Eve to finish a fine coat that he was supposed to deliver the next day. The tailor despaired of finishing the job and decided to go home to bed. Before he left his shop, he freed all the mice that his cat had imprisoned under-neath teacups and a bowl. During the night, while his cat bemoaned the loss of his meal of mice, the mice finished all the fine embroidery, and sewed up the remaining seams and buttons. The tailor found the coat in the morning, with a note stuck through the one unfinished buttonhole. The note read, "No more twist!"[30]

Potter had written the story in a picture letter to Freda Moore in 1901. She printed 500 copies and published the book in October 1902. In December, she sent one of the copies to Norman Warne. She wrote, "I hope that in all events you will not think the story very silly."[31]

Norman did not think the story was silly. He wanted to publish it, but felt that it was too long. Potter had included many nursery rhymes and songs, which slowed the story down. In addition, he was considering another story by Potter, one about squirrels that was based on yet another picture letter. Many letters, of the commercial variety, not picture letters, passed back and forth between Potter and Norman. By February 1903, the Frederick Warne Company had contracted to publish a shorter version of *The Tailor of Gloucester* in addition to *The Tale of Squirrel Nutkin*.

The Tailor of Gloucester was set "in the time of swords and periwigs and full-skirted coats with flowered lappets—when gentlemen wore ruffles, and gold-laced waistcoats of paduasoy and taffeta."[32] The book was very different from *The Tale of Peter Rabbit*. The main character in *The Tailor of Gloucester* was a man, a tailor. The animal characters were thoroughly integrated into human life. They walked upright, wore full sets of clothing, and lived in human houses instead of in a sandbank by a river. The clothing that the animals and the people wore reflected the time period of the book's setting. To gather ideas for her finery, for both animals and humans, Potter visited the South Kensington Museum. She learned that articles from their historical collection of garments were available for private viewing. Potter wrote, "I have been delighted to find I may draw some most beautiful 18th century clothing at S. Kensington museum, I have been looking at them for a long time in an inconvenient dark corner of the goldsmith's court, but had no idea they could be taken out of the case. The clerk says I could have any article put on a table in one of the offices; which will be most convenient."[33]

Potter used real street scenes from Gloucester, plus the interior of a real tailor's shop, with scraps and snippets of cloth littering the table. Scissors and a brass bowl of water lay on a sideboard, and tape measure, chalk, and other tools were scattered around the room. The tailor himself was shown in his trade's traditional posture, sitting cross-legged on the table, not in a chair, as he sewed.

Figure drawing had never been one of Potter's strengths. Drawing animals came much more easily to her than drawing humans. For the human figures in *The Tailor of Gloucester*, she worked from both live models and photographs in order to draw the sitting posture correctly. She had a young boy, the son of a servant, pose so that she could draw him. Her sketches showed the care she placed on details such as the position of the tailor's hands, feet, and head while sewing and, later, at rest.

For the other book that Norman wanted to publish, *The Tale of Squirrel Nutkin*, Potter used a pair of captive squirrels that she bought at a pet shop. She wrote, "I bought two but they weren't a pair, and fought so frightfully that I had to get rid of the handsomer and most savage one. The other squirrel is rather a nice little animal, but half of one ear has been bitten off, which spoils his appearance."[34] An owl, Old Brown, also figured prominently in the book. Potter went to the London Zoological Gardens to find a model for her owl.

In *The Tale of Squirrel Nutkin*, a group of squirrels voyage across a lake on rafts made of bark. They use their fluffy tails as sails to catch the wind and propel the rafts. The idea may have come from a legend from the Canadian forests, where squirrel ferries with tail sails were part of local lore. Upon reaching the island, most of the squirrels give presents to Old Brown, and ask his permission to gather nuts on his land. Only Nutkin dances up and down, rudely singing rhymes at the owl. The owl swoops down and gathers Nutkin up, intending to eat him. Nutkin sneaks off and tries to escape, but the owl catches hold of his tail. In the struggle that follows, Nutkin's tail, of which he is extremely proud due to its exceptional fluffiness and thickness, is torn off. Potter had seen a tail-less, noisy, and impertinent squirrel in Scotland in 1901. She used his cheeky posture for her drawing of Nutkin. For the setting of the lake and island, she drew the craggy countryside of

Derwentwater from Lingholm. St. Herbert's Island became Owl Island.

The Tale of Squirrel Nutkin was the first book that Potter did not print privately. With two books to come out from the Frederick Warne Company, she was very busy. Letters passed frequently between Potter and Norman. Her interest in the production of the books was detailed and thorough. The endpapers and the cloth for the binding were subject to her scrutiny.

With so much time spent on her books, Potter had less energy to devote to her parents. They expressed their displeasure with her very vocally. In August 1903, with three books in print, she wrote to Norman, "I have had such painful unpleasantness at home . . . about the work that I should like a rest from scolding while I am away. I should be obliged if you would kindly say no more about a new book at present."[35] In 1903, Potter was 37 years old, yet her parents still wanted her to travel with them, and to spend her time in London with their friends, and to go on their social calls. Most importantly, they did not want her to work. They continued to see work of all kinds, including artistic and literary expression through books, as being improper for a young woman of Potter's class.

Yet the criticisms of her parents did not cause Potter to abandon plans for more books. Her books proved to be very popular with children. By the summer of 1903, book sales were so good that she received an unexpectedly large check from the Frederick Warne Company. She wrote to Norman, acknowledging his success in his bookselling trips, "It seems a great deal of money for such little books. I cannot help thinking it is a good deal owing to your spreading them about so well." She added, "It is pleasant to feel I could earn my own living."[36] Potter's desire for independence and self-expression overcame her parents' objections. She was also developing a strong friendship with the Warnes, in particular with Norman.

The Frederick Warne Company was a family-based firm. Their office was at 15 Bedford Street, in the London district known as Bloomsbury. The district was known as a center of artistic and literary activities. Virginia Woolf, a novelist; John Maynard Keynes, an economist; and Lytton Strachley,

Did you know...

The Lake District was famous in art and literature before Beatrix Potter went to live at Castle Farm. The painter Constable visited the Lake District a century before Potter went to live there. The poet William Wordsworth was a native of the area. Wordsworth always returned to the Lake District from his travels. His friend, Samuel Taylor Coleridge, lived near Wordsworth for a number of years. The poet Ruskin retired to the district, and helped raise awareness for the need to preserve the land. His house was on Lake Conniston, near the property that Potter purchased and gave to the National Trust. A friend of Potter's father, John Millais, married Ruskin's ex-wife, Effie, after her marriage to Ruskin was annulled. Millais often visited the Potter family during their vacations in Scotland and later, in the Lake District. Rupert Potter gave him many photographs, which Millais used as references in his paintings. Millais encouraged Potter's interest in art and illustration.

a historian, to name a few, all lived in Bloomsbury. The British Museum, with its collections of Egyptian and Greek antiquities, medieval English artifacts, and much more, was a few blocks away from the Warne family's home.

The widow of the founder, Louisa Warne, lived around the corner from the office in the family house at 8 Bedford Square, with her unmarried son Norman, and his likewise unmarried sister Amelia, called Mille or Old Mill. The Warne family was very different from the Potter family. Louisa Warne was a merry, cheerful old lady who entertained often. In addition to Norman and Amelia, she had two married sons, Harold and William Fruing, who ran the family publishing firm with Norman; and a married daughter, Edith. Children, both Louisa's own grandchildren and their friends, were in and out of her house all day. She often organized lively parties that included everyone—her children, grandchildren, and many friends of all ages. This was unlike the custom of separating adults and children that existed in Potter's family.

Norman, although somewhat shy with adults, enjoyed the company of his nieces and nephews. He collected butterflies, dressed up as St. Nick on Christmas, and built miniature houses for mice or dolls. Louisa welcomed Potter into the family circle. One day when Potter visited the family, she was offered a tour of the basement workshop where Norman built his fanciful creations. His work in progress was a magnificent redbrick villa that stood nearly four feet high. It had rooms on three floors, lace curtains in the windows, and a tower. He planned to give it to his niece Winifred. For Potter, he created a mouse house that her current pet, Hunca Munca, could inhabit.

Potter had been busy with the drawings for another rabbit story, *The Tale of Benjamin Bunny*. The story tells how Peter Rabbit's clothing, which he had lost in Mr. McGregor's garden, is recovered by Peter and his cousin Benjamin. Potter named her new character after her beloved pet from long ago, Benjamin Bouncer.

In the winter of 1903, she learned that dolls and toys representing her characters were being made without her permission. She created her own Peter Rabbit doll and registered it at the Patent Office on December 28, 1903. She worked with Norman on other Peter Rabbit merchandise, such as wallpaper, a board game, figurines, a variety of toys, and more nursery room decor.

In addition to her work on the new book and the Peter Rabbit merchandise, she had thought of an idea for a story that used Norman's dollhouse. The house had been moved to William Fruing's home in the town of Surbiton. In order that Potter could sketch the doll house, William Fruing invited her to visit and have lunch. There was an obstacle, however. Potter's mother objected to her daughter's now-frequent visits to the Warne house. She felt that her daughter, being from the upper classes, should not be so familiar with a family of what she called "tradespeople," that is, people who ran small businesses or who owned shops. She forbade Potter from visiting William Fruing's family in Surbiton. As Potter wrote, "My mother is so exacting I had not enough spirit to say anything about it. I have felt vexed with myself since, but did not know what to do. It does wear a person out . . . People who only see her casually do not know how disagreeable she can be when she takes dislikes."[37] Potter had to rely on photographs of the doll house for her sketches.

The story of the dollhouse involved not only the dolls living in the house, but also mice. The dolls, Lucinda and Jane, go for a drive. While they are gone, two mice, Tom

Thumb and his wife Hunca Munca, invade the empty house. The mice become incensed when they are not able to eat any of the dolls' food. The food is made of plaster. They go on a rampage and tear apart the dolls' furniture, until they realize that they can carry the bedclothes and a cradle down to their own mouse hole. Lucinda and Jane are very surprised at the state of their house when they return, but, "neither of them made any remark."[38]

With some revision, *Benjamin Bunny* and *The Tale of Two Bad Mice* were sent to the printers. For her next book, Potter thought of an unusual animal to be her heroine. It would be a hedgehog named Mrs. Tiggy-Winkle. Her own hedgehog, Tiggy, was a favorite pet. Hedgehogs were indigenous to the British Isles and Europe, but not to America. They were tiny creatures, about the size of a mole, which bore spines like a porcupine. They rolled themselves tightly into a ball to defend themselves.

Potter wrote, "Mrs. Tiggy as a model is comical. So long as she can go to sleep in my knee she is delighted, but if she is propped up on end for half an hour, she first begins to yawn pathetically, and then she *does* bite! Nevertheless she is a dear person; just like a very fat, rather stupid little dog."[39]

Potter solved the problem of getting Tiggy to pose by making a dummy, which could be dressed in petticoats and a wash apron. In *The Tale of Mrs. Tiggy-Winkle*, Tiggy was to appear as a washerwoman, modeled both on the pet hedgehog and a Scottish laundress named Kitty MacDonald who Potter had known at Dalguise House in Scotland. For her illustrations, Potter used not only her pet hedgehog and her memories of Kitty MacDonald, but also the interiors of farm kitchens in the Lake Country around Sawrey.

Potter's pet Hunca Munca came to a sad end. As a present to Potter, Norman had built a mouse house for Hunca

Beatrix Potter farmed in the Lake District of England for over thirty years, during which time she often used her surroundings as inspiration for her books. Her love for nature and animals of all sorts can be seen clearly in her books. Potter sat atop this hill on her land and sketched scenery of the village of Sawrey as seen in the photograph above.

Munca. On July 21, 1905, Potter wrote to Norman, "I cannot forgive myself for letting her tumble. I do miss her so. She fell off the chandelier, she managed to stagger up the staircase into your little house, but she died in my hand about 10 minutes after. I think if I had broken my own neck it would have saved a great deal of trouble."[40]

Within days of her letter about Hunca Munca's death, Potter received a letter from Norman. This letter was not about page proofs or endpapers or book binding. Norman wrote to Potter to ask for her hand in marriage. Their friendship had deepened into love. She accepted, and they exchanged rings.

Potter's father and mother were furious. They refused to accept Norman as a son-in-law, and they forbad Potter to marry him. She was 39 and legally able to make decisions on her own. She made it clear that she intended to marry Norman. For the sake of peace in the family, she agreed to a secret engagement, with no announcement to anyone other than family members.

The engagement did not last long, and the marriage never occurred. Norman, whose health had been delicate, became ill and died within a month of the engagement. He had either pernicious anemia or leukemia. The diagnosis was not clear, but there was no treatment for either disease at the time. He was 37 years old.

Potter felt his death keenly. Norman's sharp editorial eye had made their work together on the books into an artistic partnership. The sudden opening of hope, hope for a marriage, hope for a life with the companionship of a husband, hope for a future with a helpmate to support and encourage her, all of these hopes were dashed. She wrote to Norman's brother, Harold, "I feel as if my work and your kindness will be my greatest comfort."[41] For work, she had her books, the merchandising of products related to her books, and her longtime interest in mycology.

Potter had a new interest as well. She had purchased a field in 1903, near her favorite village in the Lake District, the village of Sawrey. By the summer of 1905, before Norman's death, the sales of her books and a small legacy gave her the financial means to buy a farm, complete with farmhouse, animals, and even a farm dog. The property was called Hill Top Farm. It had been rented to a tenant farmer, who agreed to stay and manage the farm. Hill Top Farm was the farm that Potter had described when she wrote about her sadness at leaving Don the farm dog. Now the farm was hers. It remained her property for the rest of her life.

In 1910, Beatrix Potter purchased Castle Farm, whose fields were next to those of Hill Top Farm. When she married William Heelis in 1913, Potter moved from the farmhouse on Hill Top Farm into the larger Castle Cottage (shown above) on Castle Farm.

5

Politics and Marriage

THE FARM AND her work on books provided a small amount of comfort to Potter in the months following Norman's death. She had hoped to move into her own household when she married Norman. However, as an unmarried woman, even a successful one in her late thirties, her parents refused to allow her the independence of living in a home of her own. Potter herself had a strong sense of daughterly duty, despite her parents' overbearing and controlling attitude toward her. To them, Hill Top Farm was little more than a hobby, a financial speculation, an investment property in a region where land values had remained very strong over the years.

Potter's view of Hill Top Farm was dramatically different from that of her parents. Like Bertram, who had moved to Scotland full-time, she wanted to live on a working farm. She did not, however, want to be a country lady, afraid to get her hands dirty. She wanted to participate in the day-to-day farming life, helping to birth the lambs, tend the horses, and take care of the pigs.

Potter was fortunate in that the tenant farmer, John Cannon, who had rented Hill Top Farm from the previous owner, agreed to stay and manage the farm. He had feared, when the farm was sold, that he would be given notice, that is, that he would be laid off. If Potter had given him notice, he would have had to find a new farming job and move his family. Instead, Potter asked him to assess the value of all the tools and farm stock that he had brought with him to Hill Top Farm. When she saw the painstaking fairness with which he undertook to assign a price to each bit of his property, she knew two things about him. First, she knew that he was an honest man who did not exaggerate his price, but one who took infinite care not to overcharge her by a single penny. Second, by going over his assessment in detail, and by discussing how he arrived at his valuation, she learned that he was very knowledgeable about farming and about farming in the Lake District in particular. She valued his honesty and his knowledge. She asked him to stay at Hill Top Farm as her "hind,"[42] as a farm manager was called in Sawrey.

Potter fell ill again during the winter, weakened by the events of the summer of 1905—the long battle with her parents over her engagement and its sad ending. She passed the winter at Bolton Gardens in London, where the success of *The Tale of Mrs. Tiggy-Winkle* provided relief of a sort. Thirty thousand copies of the book were sold in the first few weeks after its publication. A second book, *The Pie and the Patty Pan*, used kitchens, shop interiors and facades, and several cats that lived in Sawrey as models. When the book appeared in October 1905, Potter sent many copies to her friends in the village. A local game began, as residents tried to identify the exact location of each of the illustrations.

By spring the next year, Potter had recovered much of her strength and her spirits. The farmhouse at Hill Top Farm was too small to accommodate Potter, John Cannon, his wife, and their two small children. Potter had been staying in rented rooms in Sawrey whenever she went to visit Hill Top Farm. At last Potter decided to expand the house. She planned to add a set of rooms for the Cannon family, and to make improvements to the main house, which she would use when she stayed at the farm. It was still out of the question for her to live there full-time, but she visited as often as she could manage. When she began to remodel the house, she was able to steal away from her parents more often, as she needed to oversee the construction.

The farm expanded along with the farmhouse. In September 1906, Potter wrote, "Cannon has bought 16 ewes, so there will be lambs next spring."[43] The sheep were Herdwicks, a hardy breed that had been traditionally farmed in the hilly countryside of the Lake District. Potter's old friend, Hardwicke Rawnsley, as involved in preservation and conservation as he had always been, convinced her to buy Herdwicks, even though they were more expensive than other sheep. They were uniquely suited to the fells, as the hilly country in the Lake District was called, where open meadows were interspersed with patches of heath or poorly drained, boggy fields. Yet despite their excellent adaptation to the Lake District, Herdwicks were in danger of dying out because they were more expensive than other breeds. Rawnsley formed the Herdwick Sheepbreeders Association to maintain breeding stocks and encourage farmers to invest in the sheep. He felt that the fells in the Lake District might be abandoned as sheep farms if the traditional breed of sheep became unavailable. If that were to happen, the fells might be developed into housing for travelers, or into manufacturing areas. He

Did you know...

Beatrix Potter's parents did not want her to marry Norman Warne because he was "in trade," that is, he worked in publishing. Yet Rupert and Helen Potter were the children of families that had made fortunes in the cotton industry. Potter's parents viewed social class very narrowly, so that even the owner of a company, like Norman, was not seen as the equal of a lawyer like Rupert. Later, they disapproved of Potter's engagement to William Heelis, although he was a lawyer too. The English legal profession was split into separate branches. Rupert was a barrister, that is, he was allowed to argue cases in court. Heelis was a solicitor, who prepared briefs and gave legal advice on contracts. He did not appear in court cases. This narrow view of their social class made it difficult for Potter and her brother Bertram to find people their parents deemed suitable for marriage.

felt that the land was best used in the traditional way, in sheep farming.

Potter, with her interest in farming sparked by her purchase of Hill Top Farm, agreed with her old friend about the value of preserving the land for agriculture. She joined the Herdwick Sheepbreeders Association and began to enter sheep from Hill Top Farm into the competitions between farmers for the best sheep of the breed.

Even with all the work involved in remodeling a farmhouse and learning about sheep breeding, Potter did not neglect her books. She had drawn frogs many times, often picturing them with fishing gear, such as rods, reels, creels, and bait. *The Tale of Mr. Jeremy Fisher*, about a frog's unsuccessful day fishing, appeared in the summer of 1906.

For Christmas, Potter designed a different sort of book with a different sort of story. One of Harold Warne's daughters, Louie, told Potter that Peter Rabbit was too nice. She wanted a story about a naughty rabbit. *The Story of a Fierce Bad Rabbit* answered her request. The book, rather than being published with a traditional binding, was printed in a panorama, or concertina format, that is, one long paper which folded up into the size of a book. The story is much simpler, with less text, than any of the tales that Potter had written previously. She intended it for younger children, children who might be able to read a sentence, but not a whole paragraph. Another concertina book, *The Story of Miss Moppet*, was also a very simple story with limited text.

The Tale of Tom Kitten, published in 1907, returned to the droll characterizations of animals as small children that had been so popular in Peter Rabbit. With guests expected for tea, Mrs. Tabitha Twitchit dressed her kittens Tom, Mittens, and Moppet in their finest clothing and warned them to remain presentable. Tom's clothing did not stay on, because he had gotten so fat that the buttons burst off. The other kittens did not stay clean or walk on their hind legs to protect their good clothes, no matter who was coming to tea. The kittens, in fact, lost all their clothes, which were then put on by Mr. Drake Puddle-Duck and his family. Of course, when the Puddle-Duck family went swimming on the duck pond, all of the garments came off because they had no buttons. The ducks "have been looking for them ever since."[44] The illustration facing this last page in the book showed the duck family, bottoms up, searching the duck pond for the lost clothing.

Harold Warne, as Potter's editor, tried to get her to change some of the wording in *The Tale of Tom Kitten*. He felt that it might not be suitable to say "all his clothes came off" in a book meant for children. Potter protested, "'*Nearly* all' won't do! because I have drawn Thomas already with *nothing*! That would not signify; I could gum [draw] something over but there are not many garments for Mr. Drake to dress himself in; and it would give the story a new & criminal aspect if he forcibly took and *stole* Tom's trousers!"[45]

The exterior view of the farmhouse at Hill Top Farm and various scenes in the gardens appear in the illustrations of *The Tale of Tom Kitten*. The farm had many cats, brought by Mrs. Cannon to try to control the abundance of rats that infested the house and barn. As Potter noted, "The rats have come back in great force, two big ones were trapped in the shed here, beside turning out a nest of eight baby rats in the cucumber frame opposite the door. They are getting at the corn at the farm. Mrs. Cannon calmly announced that she should get four or five cats! . . . Mrs. Cannon has seen a rat sitting up eating its dinner under the kitchen table in the middle of the afternoon. We are putting zinc on the bottoms of the doors—that and cement skirtings will puzzle them."[46]

For her next book, *The Tale of Jemima Puddle-Duck*, Potter painted the landscape across Esthwaite Water, with Jemima flying over it. Potter's dog Kep became the hero, rescuing Jemima from the "foxy gentleman" who actually was a fox. As Potter-biographer Judy Taylor noted in the critical essay *The Little Books*, the foxy gentleman "was Beatrix's favorite villain: a silver-tongued charmer who, laying a finger to his nose, invites Jemima to make free use of his summer residence for her nest, plotting a vulpine version of *droit du seigneur* [ravishment]."[47] The book also showed Mrs. Cannon standing at the farmhouse door, feeding the poultry.[48]

Potter depicted herself in *The Roly-poly Pudding* (later retitled *The Tale of Samuel Whiskers*). Published in 1908, the book showed Tom Kitten being captured by the evil rat Samuel Whiskers, who, with his wife Anna Maria, rolled Tom in a crust with the intent to bake him alive. The book showed the farm kitchen of Hill Top Farm, the old iron stove, and the staircase.

One of the rats at Hill Top Farm became something of a pet for Potter, although she did not trap him or keep him in a cage. She wrote, "He had stolen the oddest thing! There is a sort of large cupboard or closet where I do my photograph-ing, it is papered inside with rather a pretty green and gold paper; and Samuel had torn off strips of paper all round the closet as high as he could reach up. I could see the marks of his little teeth! Every scrap was taken away. I wonder what in the world he wanted if for? I think Anna Maria must have been there, with him, to help, and I think she must have wanted to paper her best sitting room!"[49]

Eventually, at least in the book, Samuel Whiskers and Anna Maria run away from the farm, with their belongings in a wheelbarrow. The figure of a lady, believed to be Potter, watches from a distance as they scamper along.

Beatrix Potter lived all of her married life at Castle Cottage, shown above, nestled among the trees. She loved to roam the countryside around her farm, observing the dogs, ponies, and other creatures of the outdoors. Living on the farm gave her the opportunity to resume her childhood study of fungi, given up after she realized she would never be taken seriously in the scientific world because she was female.

The popularity of these books created an opportunity for tie-ins based on the characters. Potter earned a royalty on the sale of all the licensed merchandise. She was very concerned with the quality of the products that were related to her books. With every doll, tea set, game, wallpaper pattern, or china figurine, Potter insisted that the materials be high quality and that the characters be represented accurately. She had a shrewd estimation for what products would be popular, and how much to charge for them. Her royalties from the books and the product tie-ins brought her enough money to buy more land near Hill Top Farm.

Her lawyer, William Heelis, helped her find and acquire properties. The youngest of 12 children, Heelis was in his forties and unmarried. He was a specialist in the sale of farm properties, knowing land, building, and stock valuation. Over the years, their business relationship became a warm friendship.

Yet Potter was still not free to spend her days exclusively at Hill Top Farm as she wanted to do. Her parents suffered one health complaint after another. They expected Potter to help with the management of their household at Two Bolton Gardens and to nurse them through their various illnesses. Although she had a dozen books in print in English, with translations into French and German on the way, as well as a multitude of products, her parents still viewed Potter as their spinster daughter. While she did her best to satisfy their demands and her own conscientious feelings of duty towards them, her own health suffered. She often fell ill in the winters, and the springs and summers in the countryside did nothing to improve her health.

In the years between 1908 and 1913, Potter published seven books: *The Tale of the Flopsy Bunnies*; *Ginger and Pickles*; *The Tale of Mrs. Tittlemouse*; *The Tale of Timmy Tiptoes*; *Peter Rabbit's Painting Book*; *The Tale of Mr. Tod*; and *The Tale of Pigling Bland*.

For the last book, Potter again turned to a pet as a personality in the story. When she bought it, Hill Top Farm had no pigs. John Cannon, the farm manager, often pointed out to Potter that most farms in the neighborhood had at least a few pigs. He convinced her to buy several. He was very particular about the animals that he purchased. He always insisted on knowing the pedigree of any pig before he would consider buying it.

One litter that he bought had a tiny black female pig, the runt, which normally would not have been included in the sale. Potter, however, seeing the tiny sow, insisted on bringing it home. She named it Pig Wig and made it into a pet. Pig Wig slept in a basket by Potter's bed. Potter fed her pet with a bottle until Pig Wig was ready for solid food. Pig Wig appeared as the beautiful black girl-pig in the *Tale of Pigling Bland*.[50]

Potter's interest in the Lake District led her to political activism. One of Potter's political activities was a campaign in 1912 against the noise and danger of landing flying boats on Lake Windermere, the largest natural lake in England and one of the most beautiful lakes in the world. A factory for building flying boats was planned for the Lake District. Potter's letter-writing campaign and the number of signatures she obtained on a petition against the factory led to the idea's abandonment.

Another of her political interests was the question of free trade. Her own business had suffered when cheap imported toys were marketed in Britain. Without a tariff, or tax on imports, her high-quality merchandise did not sell as well as the foreign toys. She produced, at her expense, a series of pamphlets, advertisements, and mailings that opposed free trade and called for protection of British goods by means of a tariff. Unfortunately, her cause failed in the general election of 1910.

The year before the election, Potter had bought Castle Farm. Its fields were adjacent to Hill Top Farm, and the farmhouses were "within whistling distance."[51] Her lawyer, William Heelis, helped her buy Castle Farm. Potter decided to make improvements to the farm, beginning with the addition of running water to the farmhouse. They inspected the work often, and spent a great deal of time together. Heelis was a tall, attractive man, with a gentle, courteous manner. Potter caught cold during one of the tours of the construction at Castle Farm. She was forced by her ill health to go to her parents' London home, where the cold threatened to turn into influenza. Heelis wrote many letters to her, keeping her informed about news from Sawrey and about the improvements at Castle Farm. His letters kept her from the usual problems which affected her disposition when she was at Two Bolton Gardens, namely, loneliness and depression. In one letter, he asked her to marry him.

Potter's parents were again opposed to the marriage, feeling that Heelis, as a country lawyer, was of a lower social class than their daughter. Even though she was in her forties, she found it difficult to go against their wishes. She was so concerned about their opposition that her convalescence was slow and difficult.

An unexpected ally came forward to help her: her brother Bertram. He revealed to them that he had been secretly married for seven years. He had kept his marriage secret from his parents because he did not want to face the conflicts that he knew they would create. He had married a woman of a different social class. With her brother's support, and with her own growing determination to seek happiness, Potter won her parents' consent to marry. She and Heelis were married on October 14, 1913. They went to live at Castle Cottage on Castle Farm.

Beatrix Potter wrote many lengthy letters throughout her life. In fact, the original idea of The Tale of Peter Rabbit *(including small drawings) first appeared in a "picture letter" she wrote to Noel Moore, the son of her second governess Annie (Carter) Moore. Many of her letters and writings (some of which are shown above) are now on display at her former home on Hill Top Farm in the Lake District of England.*

Preserving the Land

POTTER AND WILLIAM Heelis, known as Willie, moved into the cottage at Castle Farm once the renovations were completed. Although she was married and the owner of her own home, Potter still traveled to London frequently, to take care of her parents. Her father was ill the winter of 1913, and died in May of the next year. Potter found a home for her mother near Sawrey, so that she could care for her aging mother without making the long train trip to London.

World events, in addition to the loss of her father, made 1914 a difficult year for Potter. Archduke Franz Ferdinand, heir to the throne of Austria-Hungary, was assassinated on July 28 in Sarajevo. Sarajevo was the capitol of what was then the state of Bosnia-Herzegovina. The assassination of the archduke precipitated World War I. Emperor Franz Josef, Franz Ferdinand's father, believed that the leaders of the neighboring state of Serbia were responsible for the conspiracy that caused his son's death. He asked them to turn over the members of the assassination conspiracy to his government. When the demand was refused, Austria-Hungary declared war on Serbia. The tangled web of international alliances caused Germany, France, Russia, Italy, Great Britain, and eventually the United States and many other nations, to join the war.

By some estimates, over 8.5 million soldiers died during World War I, with over 21 million wounded. Britain alone suffered nearly one million deaths in her armed forces, with over two million wounded.[52] Armed blimps known as Zeppelins crossed the English Channel and dropped bombs on London as well as other places in England and Scotland. With civilians being killed on British soil, the country mobilized for the defense at home as well as for warfare abroad.

Many men went into the armed services, so fewer laborers were available to work on farms. The government increased the amount of paperwork for farmers, and requisitioned (took for military use) some of Potter's horses. The lack of labor, both on farms and in the weapons industries, led many employers to offer positions to women. War work, as it was called, brought many women their first nondomestic jobs.

Few families were unaffected by the war. Most Britons lost sons or cousins or nephews. Potter lost a distant set of cousins when the passenger liner *Lusitania* was torpedoed by German U-boats (early submarines). The British government insisted that the ship was unarmed, and that it carried no munitions or war materials. Over 1,000 civilians (passengers and crewmembers) were killed. The attack on the *Lusitania* was one of the events that helped to convince the United States to join the war.

Christmas 1914 was the first year in more than a decade without the publication of a new book by Potter. She found that her new freedom, as a married woman independent of her parents, absorbed most of her energy. Farming, she found, was a full-time occupation. In addition, her eyesight had been strained by so much work on tiny pictures.

The royalties from her existing works over the war years trickled in very slowly from Potter's publisher. She wrote several times requesting an accounting of the payments, but her requests were never fully satisfied. In 1917, Harold Warne was arrested and charged with embezzlement. He was convicted and sentenced to prison. He had been transferring money from the publishing side of the business into an ailing fishing subsidiary. His brother, William Fruing, restructured the company. In the process, he had to sell his home. His family moved into a smaller, cheaper lodging, with some of the servants who agreed to work for room and board, without wages. All the furniture from the home, including the dollhouse which Norman had made for William Fruing's children, and which Potter had drawn in *The Tale of Two Bad Mice*, was sold.

Potter, throughout the financial troubles, remained a solid friend to the Warnes, writing sympathetically to her friend Millie and to William Fruing's children. In turn, William Fruing made sure that Potter's books and her financial interests in the merchandise tie-ins were protected when he reorganized the company. To help bring in money, William Fruing asked if Potter would be interested in publishing a new book. Although she told him that her eyesight had become too strained for a completely new book, she did have an idea. She suggested an old project, that of an illustrated set of nursery rhymes. She had proposed *Appley Dapply's Nursery Rhymes* soon after the publication of *The Tale of Peter Rabbit* in 1902, but Norman had been more interested in story books than in nursery rhymes. Potter, however, had continued to write and illustrate nursery rhymes over the years. *Appley Dapply*, published in 1917, was a compilation of the illustrated rhymes Potter had collected.

The war dragged on through most of 1918. War news was tragic, telling stories of many men being slaughtered in order to advance a few miles into enemy territory. Heelis, even though he was in his forties, received his call-up papers. When he reported for his physical, however, his health was not good enough for him to be drafted. Soon after that piece of good news, however, Potter received word that her brother Bertram had died suddenly of a hemorrhage. He was only 46.

Potter wrote to her friend Hardwicke Rawnsley about Bertram's death. "These sudden calls are very merciful, but a shock. And hard to realize; I don't think I yet realize that Bertram is gone—in his prime, and in his usefulness. He had such a fine farm . . . I do think he found true happiness in hard useful manual work. It is good to remember how much more cheerful & contented he had seemed towards the last. He had not painted lately, but he hoped & intended to take it up again 'after the war.' He is buried . . . in the bend of a stream—a flowery graveyard with a ruined ivy grown church . . ."[53]

Potter's new book, *The Tale of Johnny Town Mouse*, published in 1918. It was the last of her small-format story books. Even with spectacles, which she began to wear that year, she felt that the details of working on the illustrations for the small books were beyond her abilities. Her interests also had changed. Beatrix Potter the artist and writer transformed herself into Beatrix Heelis, the farmer.

During the war, there were occasional shortages of feed for the farm animals. The wife of a local farmer remembered her husband's story of having seen Potter:

> . . . when food was scarce . . . [the farmer] came upon her one wet cold November day gathering acorns in the woods for her pigs. She had a shovel and a wheelbarrow for the job, and was fit up to brave the weather in short thick wool skirt, a man's jacket and cap and a sack over her shoulders . . . She was on the Graythwaite side of Esthwaite Lake and would have to wheel that heavy barrow up a long steep hill home just to give the animals she loved a treat.[54]

Potter roamed the countryside, sometimes keeping watch over her sheep, sometimes merely observing the dogs, ponies, and other creatures of the fells. She wore warm, comfortable, but sometimes outlandish garb. Her favorite shoes were clogs, similar to the ones her character Peter Rabbit had lost in Mr. McGregor's garden. The clogs were practical footwear for a farmer, as they were metal-soled, but had supple leather uppers. They could be kicked off easily, so that mud (so often mixed with manure when walking around a farm) was not tracked into the house. Potter's favorite tweed skirts and jackets were woven from the wool of her own sheep. Yet sometimes her layers of clothing, worn to protect her from the damp and cold weather, were a source of amusement. She told the story of one wet, windy day when she was out checking on the lambs. She met a tramp as she walked a steep road to the pasture. He called out to her, evidently mistaking her for a homeless person like himself, "It's sad weather for the likes o'thee and me!"[55]

Just as she had once taken an interest in mushrooms and had taught herself virtually everything there was to know about them, so Potter applied herself to farming in general and sheep in particular. To protect the sheep from parasites, she invented a trap for the maggot-flies that tormented them. She thought it would be more useful to trap the flies than to try to exterminate them by dipping the sheep into pesticides. Her trap was used in large numbers by the sheep farmers in the fells.[56]

On November 11, 1918, a truce was declared. All the parties involved in the war laid down their weapons at 11:11 A.M. on that day. The peace that ensued only lasted 20 years. The Treaty of Versailles gave the French territory that the Germans felt was theirs by right. The Germans were also forced to pay reparations (payments of damages), which they felt were unfair. With the coming of the Great Depression, Germany was ready for a strong political leader. Adolf Hitler claimed to be such a leader. His National Socialist Party came to power in 1933.

In the decade after World War I ended, Potter published *Cecily Parsley's Rhymes* (1922), another compilation of nursery rhymes, and two books derived from previous stories, *Jemima Puddle-Duck's Painting Book* (1925) and *Peter Rabbit's Almanac* (1929). *Cecily Parsley's Rhymes* was a sequel to *Appley Dapply's Nursery Rhymes*. *Jemima Puddle-Duck's Painting Book* and *Peter Rabbit's Almanac* were intended to begin two new series of books, but the work on those series took time away from working the farm, so Potter never continued them.

With the restructuring of the Frederick Warne Company after Harold Warne's embezzlement, Potter began to see an increase in her royalties. Her books sold well, and product tie-ins, such as the dolls of her characters, were a strong source of income. As properties became available in the Lake District, Potter bought them. She was very active in keeping land for farming.

One of the farms that Potter bought was Troutbeck Farm, which came onto the market in 1923. At 2,000 acres, with

Beatrix Potter was interested in preserving the lands in the Lake District of England. She didn't want the farmland to become overdeveloped. To that end, Potter bought land as it became available and maintained it as farmland. She worked hard to raise Herdwick sheep (pictured here), which were more expensive, but were particularly suited to the land of the Lake District of England. Over the years, many of her sheep won prizes at competitions, and more importantly, Potter came to be accepted as an equal by male farmers who had been born and raised on the land. In 1930, Potter became the first woman elected President of the Herdwick Sheep Breeders Association.

many hundred head of sheep, running Troutbeck was an ambitious undertaking. Potter loved the solitude and the scenery at Troutbeck. It was about 12 miles from Sawrey. Potter walked or drove to Troutbeck nearly every day. She wrote:

> In the midst of this waste of yellow bentgrass and stones there is a patch of green grass and a stunted thorn. Round the tree— round and round in measured canter—went four of the wild fell ponies. Round and round, then checked and turned; round and round reversed; arched necks, tossing manes, tails streaming. I watched a while crouching behind a boulder. Who had taught them? . . . Oftentimes I have seen managed horses cantering round the sawdust ring under a circus tent; but these half-wild youngsters had never been handled by man . . . While I

was watching them I remembered how I had been puzzled once before . . . In a soft muddy place. I had seen a multitude of little unshod footprints, much too small for horses' footmarks, much too round for deer or sheep . . . those little fairy footmarks . . . made me first aware of *The Fairy Caravan*.[57]

The Fairy Caravan, published in 1929, told the story of a guinea pig, Tuppenny. At the beginning of the book, Tuppenny was sickly, with patchy fur riddled with bald spots. After he was cured by a marvelous elixir, Tuppenny escaped from his owners, and joined the Fairy Caravan, a miniature traveling

Did you know...

Beatrix Potter wrote thousands of letters. Her correspondents ranged from children in foreign countries, to the Moore children, to librarians and booksellers. Several of her friends were Americans, who later sent her gifts of food and books during World War II. One of her librarian friends was Anne Carroll Moore, the Superintendent of Children's Works in the New York Public Library. Potter met Anne in 1921, when Anne came to tea at Hill Top Farm with her doll Nicholas Knickerbocker (who went everywhere she did). Moore's visit was a turning point for Potter. Although her books had always sold well, there was little public recognition of their worth. As children's books, they were not taken seriously in Britain. From Moore, Potter learned that in America, writing and illustration for children had become a respected field. A new literary magazine, *The Horn Book*, was devoted exclusively to works for children. She learned that *Appley Dapply's Nursery Rhymes* was extremely popular with the library's young patrons. Potter had become discouraged about her work, and had almost abandoned thoughts of future books. She was inspired, however, by Moore's visit. She resumed work on *Cecily Parsley's Nursery Rhymes*.

circus that visited all of the farms around Sawrey. The performers, themselves tiny animals, gave performances and told tales for the entertainment of the other creatures. The background of the pictures was Sawrey, with Potter's prize Herdwick sheep shown on the hills. The book was less successful artistically than some of her earlier work. She had used, as with her collections of nursery rhymes, many of the pictures and unpublished stories from her portfolios.

Another of the properties that Potter bought was a home, Lindeth How, which was on the far side of Lake Windermere from Castle Farm. Her family had stayed at Lindeth How several times when she was young. Even though the war was over, Potter thought that it was not a good idea for her mother to return to Two Bolton Gardens without companionship other than her servants. Potter supervised the removal of furniture, china, and other items from her childhood home and her mother moved to Lindeth How. Helen lived in her new home much as she had lived in London. She spent her mornings doing embroidery, stopping for lunch at one o'clock. If the weather were fine, or if she had a call to make, she would be driven out in the afternoon in her coach. Helen lived to the age of 93. After her death, Potter wrote to Edith Rawnsley, "My mother's long life was a link with times that are passed away, though still vivid in our memory—the old leisurely pleasant days of stately carriage horses . . . Her chief interests were her canaries, her needlework and her little dog. She was wonderfully clear in mind, but . . . I am glad that she is at rest."[58]

Over the years, Potter's energetic interest in sheep farming and breeding produced excellent results. Her sheep regularly won prizes at the competitions, and she was accepted as an equal by farmers who had been born and raised in the district. In 1930, she was the first woman elected to serve as the president of the Herdwick Sheepbreeders Association.

Since Beatrix Potter's death in 1943, her books have continued to attract children and their families to the Lake District of England. In this picture we see a carriage bound for the Peter Rabbit Hotel for children at St. Annes-on-the-Sea. The Lake District of England provides tours of Potter's home and museum.

7

Potter's Legacy

POTTER'S WORK PRESERVING farmland and working on her own farm continued during the 1930s. She increased her personal landholdings, and worked with the National Trust to acquire property on its behalf. Her income from her previously published books remained strong, as the books continued to be translated into many languages. By 1934, *The Tale of Peter Rabbit* had appeared in six languages in addition to English. At the beginning of the decade, Potter published two more original works.

The Tale of Little Pig Robinson appeared in 1930. Although the story of Pig Robinson had been written in 1883, the Frederick Warne Company had not been interested in publishing it previously. There were a few watercolor paintings at the beginning of the book, which showed the village and Pig Robinson as he set out on his adventures. The rest of the illustrations were black-and white drawings.

There are subtle and not-so-subtle hints of her other books throughout *The Tale of Little Pig Robinson*. The story tells how Pig Robinson is waylaid, like David Balfour in the book *Kidnapped* by Robert Louis Stevenson. Pig Robinson's kidnapper is a ship's cook, who takes him on board. The cook feeds him muffins and crumpets until Pig Robinson, stuffed with sweets, falls asleep. When he awakens, he is far out at sea. The ship's cat helps Pig Robinson escape from being cooked for the Captain's birthday dinner. Pig Robinson, like the title character in Daniel Defoe's book, *Robinson Crusoe*, ended up on a deserted isle. Unlike Crusoe, however, Pig Robinson receives visitors on his island, where the Bong tree grows. Some of the guests are the Owl and the Pussycat, who had set to sea in a pea-green boat in another children's story, Edward Lear's *The Owl and the Pussycat*.

The Tale of Little Pig Robinson is a chapter book, and its length, coupled with the lack of colored illustrations, had caused it to be rejected by the Frederick Warne Company in the past. However, when it was finally published, the book did well in both the United States and England.

The income from *The Tale of Little Pig Robinson* was immediately used to purchase land. An enormous holding, Monk Conniston Estate, had come onto the market. At 4,000 acres, it was twice the size of Troutbeck Farm.

Potter wanted the land to be kept intact, with its farms and cottages preserved. If one person wasn't able to buy the whole tract of land, there was a danger that the holding would be broken up and the land taken out of farming. Part of the land had once been owned by one of Potter's ancestors. "I am very interested because my great grand-father had land there and I always longed to buy it back and give it to the National Trust in remembrance. I was very much attached to my grandmother Jessy Crompton and said to be very like her, 'only not so good-looking!!' according to old folks. Perhaps I will be able to help out of this book [*The Tale of Little Pig Robinson*]—it would be like a fairy tale, would it not?"[59]

Potter's fairy tale came true. She bought the estate, and offered half of it to the Trust immediately at the price she paid for it. They raised the money swiftly. She promised the rest of the land to them in the future. The managers of the Trust, appreciating Potter's reputation as a farmer, asked her to manage the entire property.

Life for Potter was more than farming and property management. A new fad had sprung up in the county, that of folk dancing. She often went with Heelis to the dances, but Potter stayed on the sidelines. She described the dancing and the festivities that accompanied them, "The plum cake and laughter. Fat and thin, and high and low, the nimble and the laggard, the toddler and the grey-haired gran—all dancing with a will."[60]

Potter's interest in children remained strong. She invited groups of Girl Guides to camp on her property. If the weather turned rainy, she let them stay in the farm buildings at Troutbeck or her other properties. Heelis's young nieces and nephews also came to stay with them at Castle Farm. Furthermore, Potter had many pen friends all over the world,

Beatrix Potter's books have never been out of print. Her stories have been made into animated features, movies, plays, and ballets. Pictured here is a Royal Ballet production of **Tales of Beatrix Potter** *from 1992.*

who treasured her letters the same way the Moore children had treasured her original picture letters.

The book *Sister Ann*, published in 1932, was an adaptation of the grisly tale *Bluebeard*. Although it had been originally intended as part of *The Fairy Caravan*, *Sister Ann* was too long to be included. When it was published Potter did not illustrate the book. Her eyesight, and her many other occupations, made it impossible for her to illustrate her own work as she had always done in the past.

In 1936, a letter arrived at Castle Farm. It contained an offer from Walt Disney, who wanted to make an animated feature about *The Tale of Peter Rabbit*. Potter felt that her drawings would not look good on the silver screen. She said, "To make Silly Symphonies like the movie *Fantasia*, which was based in part on symphonic music they will have to enlarge them and that will show up all the imperfections."[61]

Potter's health began to fail, making it difficult for her to do the outdoor work she enjoyed so much. Her tendency to suffer from colds and influenza in the winter kept her off the fells, and indoors. She went into the hospital for a minor gynecological problem, and ended up having two surgeries. Her vivid imagination gave her comfort when she was ill. She wrote, ". . . as I lie in bed I can walk step by step on the fells and rough lands seeing every stone and flower and patch of bog and cotton pass where my old legs will never take me again. Also, do you not feel it is rather pleasing to be so much wiser than quantities of young idiots?"[62]

The year 1939 saw the beginning of World War II. Anticipating raids from planes instead of Zeppelins this time, the country prepared for war. Blackout drills were held, to prevent planes from being able to find British cities, factories, or bridges. Because there were no global positioning systems, computers, or accurate celestial navigation instruments at that time, the home defense forces relied on keeping the cities and the countryside in complete darkness. Without light from the ground to guide them, enemy planes had to use starlight or moonlight to find their way across the English Channel and towards their targets.

After war was declared, many buildings and houses were commandeered by the army to use as staff headquarters. One of Potter's cousins, Sir William Hyde-Parker, wrote to Potter that his home, Medford Hall, had been taken over by the army. He asked if he and his family could live at one of her properties. She had often stayed at Medford Hall, and had made many sketches of the gardens surrounding it. Potter invited Sir William to stay at Hill Top Farm. Hill Top Farm had been her sanctuary, where her drawings and her painting studio were located. She boxed up her treasures, and gave it to her cousin for the duration of the war.

In June 1940, the British retreated from Europe after having suffered devastating losses in Flanders. The evacuation at Dunkirk, where a multitude of boats rescued the British Expeditionary Forces as well as the remnants of the French Army, caused anxiety throughout the country. Fears were high that the German Army might cross the Channel and invade England. Of Britain's strength and her resolution to continue the fight, even if the British were fighting alone, Prime Minister Winston Churchill said, "Let us therefore brace ourselves to our duties, and so bear ourselves that if the British Empire and Commonwealth last for a thousand years, men will still say, This was their finest hour." [63] Many British citizens, including Potter, were very angry at the United States for remaining neutral in the conflict. The United States did not declare war until after the attack on Pearl Harbor, on December 7, 1941.

Food shortages were common during the war. Potter had received packages of books from her pen pals over the years. Now they began to send her food. Fruit juices were particularly in short supply. Potter wrote, "Your charming present arrived unexpectedly this morning—*Lemon Juice!* . . . It helped my cough when I had bronchitis all through the month of May . . . I am not coughing now, so I shall save your lemon juice till next winter." [64]

Despite paper shortages, the Frederick Warne Company continued printing all of Potter's books. One entire edition of *The Tale of Peter Rabbit* was lost, however, when the printers in London suffered a direct hit from a bomb. The original watercolors for the books were sent to Sawrey for safekeeping. "No place is safe," Potter wrote, "but the chances of any individual house being hit is small in the country . . . There were bombers over head all night long, we are on a bombing 'route' here, they fly over and come back; and to judge by the noise some go lost and wander round."[65]

The Girl Guides camped on Potter's land during the summers while the war raged. Some of them were from the inner cities, and had not gotten enough to eat. Potter made sure they were well fed when they were at camp. She gave them the fresh milk and eggs that they needed, as well as fresh mutton from her herds. One group of Guides, learning that Potter's seventy-seventh birthday was on July 27, 1943, organized a party for her. They went to greet her at Castle Farm dressed as characters from her books. Potter enjoyed the occasion very much, and gave away so many

Did you know...

In addition to the land she donated or sold to the National Trust during her lifetime, over 2,000 acres were given to the Trust upon Beatrix Potter's death. The National Trust was founded in 1895 by three visionary philanthropists—Miss Octavia Hill, Sir Robert Hunter, and Potter's friend, Hardwicke Rawnsley. Concerned about the impact of uncontrolled development and the rapid industrialization of the countryside, they set up the National Trust to act as a guardian in the acquisition and protection of threatened coastal properties, farm lands, and historic buildings.

autographed copies of her books that she had to order more from her publisher.

Potter was ill with bronchitis again during the winter of 1943. Her heart had never been quite normal after the rheumatic fever she had suffered as a girl. That winter, her heart gave her increasing trouble. She died on December 22, 1943. Her body was cremated, and her ashes were scattered on her beloved fells.

Potter left her estate to Heelis for his lifetime, with the bulk of her estate to go to the National Trust upon his death. She also gave him a choice of properties to bequeath as he chose. Rather than leave the properties to his relatives, Heelis left it all to the National Trust. He died barely two years after his wife.

Hill Top Farm became a museum housing Potter's possessions, such as her collection of china figurines and her furniture. Everything was left in place to show what it had been like when Potter lived there. In addition, Heelis's law office building in Hawkshead was given to the National Trust. It became a museum that housed exhibitions of Potter's original drawings. Thousands of tourists visited the farm and museum every year.

Potter's legacy remained multifold. Her efforts to preserve farming led to about one-quarter of the land in the Lake District, where Hill Top Farm was located, being conserved in perpetuity as farmland. The National Trust has become a model for saving land from development throughout the world.

Potter's books have never been out of print. Her stories have been made into animated features, into movies, into plays, and into ballets. Many toys and other merchandise (tea sets, dolls, place mats, rugs, wallpaper, and other products) have been created based on her characters.

Potter's artistic influence was vast. She set the standard for realistic illustrations in children's books. Her belief that the text of children's books worked in tandem with the illustrations became a seminal force in children's literature.

Potter's epitaph, printed in *The New York Herald Tribune*, read:

> Beatrix Potter, North-Country farmer, connoisseur of old furniture and china, lover of nature and animals, was an artist both with words and with brush. The perfect characterizations bear witness to it and are unforgettable. Her greatness lies in the fact that she was able again and again to create that rare thing—a book that brings grown-ups and children together in a shared delight.[66]

1 Dorothy Aldis, *Nothing is Impossible: the Story of Beatrix Potter* (New York: Atheneum, 1969), 19–20.

2 Ibid., 33–34.

3 Ibid., 36.

4 Leslie Linder, ed., *The Journal of Beatrix Potter from 1881 to 1897* (London: Frederick Warne Company, 1966), 148.

5 Aldis, 38–46.

6 Judy Taylor, *Beatrix Potter: Artist, Storyteller and Countrywoman* (London: Frederick Warne Company, 1986), 25.

7 Ibid., 21.

8 Margaret Lane, *The Tale of Beatrix Potter* (London: Frederick Warne Company, 1968), 30.

9 Linder, 338.

10 Ibid., xxiv.

11 Ibid., 147.

12 Ibid., 138.

13 Ibid., 312.

14 Margaret Lane, *The Magic Years of Beatrix Potter* (London: Frederick Warne Company, 1978), 81.

15 Linder, 205.

16 Taylor, 53.

17 Linder, 249.

18 Judy Taylor, ed., *Beatrix Potter's Letters* (London: Frederick Warne Company, 1989), 20–22.

19 Linder, 398.

20 Ibid., 375.

21 Ibid., 268.

22 Ibid., 422.

23 Ibid. 417.

24 Taylor, *Beatrix Potter: Artist, Storyteller and Countrywoman*, 71–72.

25 Lane, *The Tale of Beatrix Potter*, 62.

26 Lane, *The Magic Years of Beatrix Potter*, 99.

27 Taylor, *Beatrix Potter's Letters*, 62.

28 Lane, *The Magic Years of Beatrix Potter*, 103.

29 John Goldthwaite, *The Natural History of Make-Believe* (Oxford, UK: Oxford University Press, 1996), 287.

30 Beatrix Potter, *The Tailor of Gloucester* (London: Frederick Warne Company, 1903), 80.

31 Taylor, *Beatrix Potter's Letters*, 69.

32 Potter, *The Tailor of Gloucester*, 59.

33 Taylor, *Beatrix Potter: Artist, Storyteller and Countrywoman*, 85.

34 Lane, *The Magic Years of Beatrix Potter*, 113, 115.

35 Ibid., 115.

36 Ibid., 116.

37 Ibid., 124–125.

38 Beatrix Potter, *The Tale of Two Bad Mice* (New York: Frederick Warne Company, 1904), 64.

39 Lane, *The Magic Years of Beatrix Potter*, 132.

40 Taylor, *Beatrix Potter's Letters*, 122.

41 Ibid., 126.

42 Lane, *The Tale of Beatrix Potter*, 89

43 Taylor, *Beatrix Potter's Letters*, 147.

44 Beatrix Potter, *The Tale of Tom Kitten* (London: Frederick Warne Company, 1907), 59.

45 Taylor, *Beatrix Potter's Letters*, 150.

46 Taylor, *Beatrix Potter: Artist, Storyteller and Countrywoman*, 112.

47 Judy Taylor, et. al., *Beatrix Potter 1866-1943: The Artist and Her World* (London: Frederick Warne Company, 1987), 133.

48 Beatrix Potter, *The Tale of Jemima Puddle-Duck* (New York: Frederick Warne Company, 1910), 8.

49 Taylor, *Beatrix Potter: Artist, Storyteller and Countrywoman*, 113.

50 Ibid., 133.

51 Lane, *The Magic Years of Beatrix Potter*, 108.

52 Causalties: First World War, *www.spartacus.schoolnet.co.uk/ FWWdeaths.htm.*

53 Taylor, *Beatrix Potter's Letters*, 251.

54 Lane, *The Tale of Beatrix Potter*, 143.

55 Ibid., 150.

56 Ibid.

57 Ibid., 147.

58 Ibid., 145.

59 Taylor, *Beatrix Potter: Artist, Storyteller and Countrywoman*, 172.

60 Ibid., 145.

61 Ibid., 184.

62 Lane, *The Tale of Beatrix Potter*, 156–157.

63 William Churchill, Speech delivered to the House of Commons on June 18, 1940, *www.winstonchurchill.org/ i4a/pages/index.cfm?pageid =388#hour.*

64 Taylor, *Beatrix Potter: Artist, Storyteller and Countrywoman*, 198.

65 Ibid., 196.

66 Ibid., 206.

1866 Beatrix Potter born July 28.

1871 The Potter family's first summer at Dalguise House in Scotland.

1872 Bertram Potter born.

1882 Potter's first visit to the Lake District.

1883 Annie Carter becomes Potter's governess.

1885 Annie marries Edwin Moore and becomes Annie Moore.

1890 Sale of pictures to Hildesheimer & Faulkner.

1893 Potter sends a picture letter to Noel Moore, Annie's son. The letter later becomes Potter's first book *The Tale of Peter Rabbit*.

1896 Potter's first visit to Sawrey.

1897 Potter's paper "On the germination of the spores of *Agaricineae*" is read before the Linnean Society of London.

1901 *The Tale of Peter Rabbit* published privately by Potter.

1902 The Frederick Warne Company publishes their edition of *The Tale of Peter Rabbit*. *The Tailor of Gloucester* published privately by Potter.

1903 The Frederick Warne Company publishes their edition of *The Tailor of Gloucester*. *The Tale of Squirrel Nutkin* published. Potter purchases a small property near Sawrey.

1904 *The Tale of Benjamin Bunny* and *The Tale of Two Bad Mice* published.

1905 July 25, Norman Warne proposes marriage in a letter. Potter accepts. August 25, Norman Warne dies of pernicious anemia or possibly leukemia. Potter purchases Hill Top Farm. *The Tale of Mrs. Tiggy-Winkle* published.

1906 *The Tale of Mr. Jeremy Fisher*, *The Story of a Fierce Bad Rabbit*, and *The Story of Miss Moppet* published.

1907 *The Tale of Tom Kitten* published.

1908 *The Tale of Jemima Puddle-Duck*, *The Roly-poly Pudding*, and *The Tale of the Flopsy Bunnies* published.

1909 *Ginger and Pickles* published.

1910 *The Tale of Mrs. Tittlemouse* published.

1911 *The Tale of Timmy Tiptoes* and *Peter Rabbit's Painting Book* published.

1912 *The Tale of Mr. Tod* published.

1913 *The Tale of Pigling Bland* published. Potter marries William Heelis, October 14.

1917 *Appley Dapply's Nursery Rhymes* published.

1918 *The Tale of Johnny Town Mouse* published.

1922 *Cecily Parsley's Rhymes* published.

1925 *Jemima Puddle-Duck's Painting Book* published.

1929 *Peter Rabbit's Almanac* published; *The Fairy Caravan* published privately by Potter; *The Fairy Caravan* published in the United States.

1930 Elected president of the Herdwick Sheepbreeders Association. *The Tale of Little Pig Robinson* published.

1932 *Sister Ann* published.

1943 Potter dies December 22.

1944 *Wag-by Wall* published.

1956 *The Tale of the Faithful Dove* limited edition published; *The Tale of the Faithful Dove* Frederick Warne Company edition published.

1966 *The Journal of Beatrix Potter*, transcribed by Leslie Linder, published.

1989 *Beatrix Potter's Letters*, selected by Judy Taylor, published.

THE TAILOR OF GLOUCESTER

This book was Beatrix Potter's favorite. It combines a story like that of *The Elves and the Shoemaker* with a Christmas tale. Mice who have been rescued by the tailor help him finish a coat in time for delivery Christmas morning.

THE TALE OF MRS. TIGGY-WINKLE

A girl named Lucie has lost her handkerchiefs and her pinafore (apron). She sees something white in the distance, high on a hillside. She climbs up to see if she can find her missing clothing, but discovers a doorway into Mrs. Tiggy-Winkle's kitchen. Mrs. Tiggy-Winkle, a hedgehog, is in fact washing out Lucie's clothing. They set off together to deliver the washing to Mrs. Tiggy-Winkle's customers. When Lucie passes the stile (steps) to her home, she turns to thank Mrs. Tiggy-Winkle, but all she sees is the brown prickly figure of a hedgehog running away.

THE TALE OF PETER RABBIT

This book was Beatrix Potter's first published work. Initially, she published it privately, with black-and-white drawings. The Frederick Warne Company asked if they could publish an edition with watercolors. Their edition of the book, published in 1902, has never been out of print.

THE TALE OF TOM KITTEN

Plump, mischievous Tom Kitten plays in the garden wearing his fancy clothes. His buttons burst, and his clothes fall off. His mother, unwilling to have him meet her guests without his clothes, sends him upstairs with his sisters Mittens and Moppet while the guests have tea.

1901 *The Tale of Peter Rabbit* (private edition)

1902 *The Tale of Peter Rabbit* (Frederick Warne Company edition), *The Tailor of Gloucester* (private edition)

1903 *The Tailor of Gloucester* (Frederick Warne Company edition), *The Tale of Squirrel Nutkin*

1904 *The Tale of Benjamin Bunny, The Tale of Two Bad Mice*

1905 *The Tale of Mrs. Tiggy-Winkle*

1906 *The Tale of Mr. Jeremy Fisher, The Story of a Fierce Bad Rabbit, The Story of Miss Moppet*

1907 *The Tale of Tom Kitten*

1908 *The Tale of Jemima Puddle-Duck, The Roly-poly Pudding, The Tale of the Flopsy Bunnies*

1909 *Ginger and Pickles*

1910 *The Tale of Mrs. Tittlemouse*

1911 *The Tale of Timmy Tiptoes, Peter Rabbit's Painting Book*

1912 *The Tale of Mr. Tod*

1913 *The Tale of Pigling Bland*

1917 *Appley Dapply's Nursery Rhymes*

1918 *The Tale of Johnny Town Mouse*

1922 *Cecily Parsley's Rhymes*

1925 *Jemima Puddle-Duck's Painting Book*

1929 *Peter Rabbit's Almanac*

1929 *The Fairy Caravan* (privately printed), *The Fairy Caravan* (United States edition)

1930 *The Tale of Little Pig Robinson*

1932 *Sister Ann*

1944 *Wag-by Wall*

1956 *The Tale of the Faithful Dove* (limited edition), *The Tale of the Faithful Dove* (Frederick Warne edition)

1966 *The Journal of Beatrix Potter*, transcribed by Leslie Linder

1989 *Beatrix Potter's Letters*, selected by Judy Taylor

BENJAMIN BUNNY accompanies Peter Rabbit on an escapade into Mr. McGregor's garden. The two bunnies intend to rescue Peter's clothes, but become imprisoned underneath a basket for five hours. Eventually, Old Mr. Bunny frees them, but he gives them a sound whipping for having gone into the garden in the first place.

MRS. TIGGY-WINKLE the hedgehog is a washerwoman who helps a little girl named Lucie find her handkerchiefs. She was modeled after Beatrix Potter's pet hedgehog and a Scottish washerwoman named Kitty McDonald.

PETER RABBIT is the enduring favorite of all of Beatrix Potter's characters. He gets into mischief in Mr. McGregor's garden, loses his new coat and his clogs, and is almost made into a pie, like his father had been, by Mrs. McGregor. When he returns home after his adventure, he is given chamomile tea by his mother.

SQUIRREL NUTKIN is a cheeky squirrel who is unwisely impolite to Old Brown the owl, owner of Owl Island. Nutkin dances and taunts Old Brown with rude songs. Old Brown picks Nutkin up and takes him away, intending to eat him. Nutkin escapes, but in the struggle to tear himself away from Old Brown, he loses his beautiful lush tail.

THE TAILOR OF GLOUCESTER despairs of finishing a coat for delivery on Christmas Day. He returns home exhausted, unable to work any longer, but before he leaves his shop, he frees the mice that his cat Simpkin has captured under the tailor's tea cups. Simpkin, who had been saving the mice for his supper, is furious, but the mice are very grateful. They finish the coat, except for one buttonhole. When the tailor opens his shop on Christmas morning, he finds a note in the one incomplete buttonhole. It reads, "No more twist!"

TOM KITTEN is washed and dressed in his finest clothes by his mother, Tabitha Twitchit, so that he could help her greet her guests at tea. Tom, however, had gotten so plump that his coat would barely button. He played in the garden, and forgot to walk upright. When he walks on all fours, his buttons burst off, and his clothing is taken by Mr. Drake Puddle-Duck.

Beatrix Potter did not win any major awards for her books. Most of her books were published before awards such as the Whitbread or the Caldecott were established. She did, however, win a number of awards for her sheep.

Aldis, Dorothy. *Nothing is Impossible: the Story of Beatrix Potter*. New York: Atheneum, 1971.

Buchan, Elizabeth. *Beatrix Potter: the Story of the Creator of Peter Rabbit*. London: Frederick Warne Company, 1987.

Goldthwaite, John. *The Natural History of Make-Believe*. Oxford, UK: Oxford University Press, 1996.

Lane, Margaret. *The Tale of Beatrix Potter*. London: Frederick Warne Company, 1946.

————. *The Magic Years of Beatrix Potter*. London: Frederick Warne Company, 1978.

Linder, Leslie, ed. *The Journal of Beatrix Potter from 1881 to 1897*. London: Frederick Warne Company, 1966.

Taylor, Judy. *Beatrix Potter: Artist, Storyteller and Countrywoman*. London: Frederick Warne Company, 1986.

————, ed. *Beatrix Potter's Letters*. London: Frederick Warne Company, 1989.

Taylor, Judy, et. al. *Beatrix Potter 1866–1943: The Artist and Her World*. London: Frederick Warne Company, 1987.

Denyer, Susan. *At Home with Beatrix Potter: The Creator of Peter Rabbit*. New York: Harry N. Abrams, 2000.

Johnson, Jane. *My Dear Noel: the Story of a Letter from Beatrix Potter*. New York: Dial Books for Young Readers, 1999.

Potter, Beatrix. *The Art of Beatrix Potter / With an Appreciation by Anne Carroll Moore and Notes to Each Section by Enid and Leslie Linder*. London: Frederick Warne Company, 1972.

Taylor, Judy, ed. *Letters To Children From Beatrix Potter*. London: Frederick Warne Company, 1992.

www.peterrabbit.com

[World of Peter Rabbit. This is the official Beatrix Potter site created by her publisher, the Frederick Warne Company. The site features a brief biography of Potter, with notes and graphics of her work. Events of interest to Potter's readers are noted on the site. There is an on-line newsletter, a Frequently Asked Questions section, competitions, and fun facts sections.]

www.beatrixpottersociety.org.uk

[Website of the official Beatrix Potter Society, a literary and scholarly organization devoted to the study of Potter's works. Features seminars on Potter, links to exhibitions about Potter, information about her art, and ways to organize readings of her works.]

www.nationaltrust.org.uk/scripts/nthandbook.dll?ACTION= PROPERTY&PROPERTYID=148

[Web page on the National Trust site that shows the Beatrix Potter Gallery visiting information. The building that houses the library was William Heelis's law office.]

www.visitcumbria.com/bpotter.htm

[Web page on the Cumbria Tourist Association site that has information about visiting Hill Top Farm, and other Potter locations in the area. There are many links to information about Potter, as well as photos of her farms.]

www.software-technics.com/bhps/

[Website of the British Hedgehog Preservation Society, an organization dedicated to preserving hedgehogs through keeping the environment healthy, to rescuing and healing injured hedgehogs, and to helping create hedgehog-safe roads.]

MARGARET SPEAKER YUAN is the author of three biographies: *Agnes de Mille: Dancer* (Chelsea House, 1990); *Avi* (Chelsea House, 2005); and *Philip Pullman* (Chelsea House, 2005), as well as three books about world landmarks: *Royal Gorge Bridge* (Blackbirch Press, 2003); *London Tower Bridge* (Blackbirch Press, 2004); and *Arc de Triomphe* (Blackbirch Press, 2004). She is the executive director of the Bay Area Independent Publishers Association, a nonprofit organization that provides educational seminars on publishing in the San Francisco Bay area. She teaches art to children with learning disabilities, and runs writing classes for both adults and children.